A Gift of Roses

Memories of the Visit to Ireland
of the Relics of St Thérèse

DON MULLAN is the author of the acclaimed bestsellers, *Eyewitness Bloody Sunday* (Wolfhound Press, 1997), which played a crucial role in British Prime Minister Tony Blair's decision to establish a new Bloody Sunday Inquiry in 1998, and *The Dublin & Monaghan Bombings* (Wolfhound Press, 2000). Don Mullan is a native of Derry and was educated at St Joseph's Secondary School, Creggan; the Development Studies Department, Holy Ghost College, Kimmage, Dublin; and Iona College, New York. Aged fifteen, he witnessed the Bloody Sunday massacre while attending his first Northern Ireland Civil Rights march. His involvement with the Northern Ireland Civil Rights movement led him to work on civil and human rights issues around the world. In 1980, aged twenty-four, he became Director of AFrI (Action From Ireland), a Dublin-based justice, peace and human rights organisation. In 1983–4 he worked as a volunteer in Recife, Brazil. In 1994, he attended the inauguration of President Nelson Mandela, as the guest of Archbishop Tutu. He worked with Concern Worldwide for almost two years, beginning in July 1994, during which time he visited Rwanda and Zaïre. He now works as a freelance journalist/writer/broadcaster.

'Native American Thérèse' by Choctaw Artist, Gary White Deer (see p. 227).

A Gift of Roses

Memories of the Visit to Ireland
of the Relics of St Thérèse

Don Mullan

Bernie Bergin, Research Assistant

WOLFHOUND PRESS

Published in 2001 by
Wolfhound Press
An imprint of Merlin Publishing
16 Upper Pembroke Street, Dublin 2, Ireland
Tel: +353 1 676 4373; Fax: +353 1 676 4368
e-mail: publishing@merlin.ie www: merlin-publishing.com

British Library Cataloguing in Publication Data
A catalogue record for this book is available from the British Library.

ISBN 0-86327-891-4

5 4 3 2 1

Quotations from St Thérèse (pp. 32, 48, 64, 94, 108, 119, 120, 136, 143, 144, 156, 159,
160, 185, 186, 190, 238, 250, 254, 272) from Story of a Soul, translated by John Clarke, OCD
Copyright © 1975, 1976, 1996 by Washington Province of Discalced Carmelites
ICS Publications, 2131 Lincoln Road, NE Washington, DC 20002-1199, USA

Quotation from The Story of My Experiments with Truth by Mahatma Gandhi reproduced
courtesy of Arun Gandhi.

Royalties from this book will be donated to the Louis and Zelie Martin Foundation.

Frontispiece: Painting of St Thérèse by Gary White Deer
Photographs: Pictures of St Thérèse (pp. 3, 6, 94 and 144) courtesy Office Central de
    Lisieux. Photograph p. 155 courtesy Dermot Beatty. All other photographs courtesy
    David Stephenson
Cover Photographs: David Stephenson
Cover Design: Slick Fish Design, Dublin
Typesetting and Book Design: Emer Ryan
Printed in the Republic of Ireland by ColourBooks, Dublin

Contents

Above: Thérèse, aged three.

Preface

Everything is Grace

This book is about the phenomenal visit of the relics of St Thérèse to our country, an attempt to evaluate what happened. Did Thérèse just come and go? The stories people are telling attest to real encounters with Thérèse; and insofar as we really did encounter her, really heard what she had to say to us and listened to it, then surely she is still here with us, in our hearts, in our lives. If we continue to listen, she will continue to speak, fulfilling her expressed desire to spend her heaven doing good on earth.

St Thérèse belongs to everyone — that was certainly demonstrated by the response the visit evoked in all quarters. But to us, her Carmelite Sisters, she is one of the family, and it was as such that we welcomed her, just as we have often been happy to welcome Sisters from other Carmelite communities. We were conscious of the fact that while she was living the Carmelite life in Lisieux, over a hundred years ago, here in Hampton our Sisters were living that same life, that same vocation, with similar desires and aspirations.

As everywhere, people came in their thousands to visit her here. The sight of all those good people coming to pray at her reliquary brought home to us anew, in a very vivid way, the power of a hidden life of prayer. Thérèse lived her few years known only to a very confined circle of people; very few beyond her family and her community were even aware of her existence, and even among that small circle fewer still suspected her sanctity. Yet, in the hundred years since she died in that total obscurity, her influence for good has spread far and wide; she has won for herself millions of friends. In innumerable ways, God has lifted the veil and shown us the seemingly limitless outreach of her life of love, prayer and sacrifice. This is what we were glimpsing as we watched, in awe, all those people coming through our little chapel, kneeling there by the reliquary in deep communion with St Thérèse, our Sister and so evidently theirs too. We were witnessing a little revelation of the power of the hidden life, right here before our eyes.

All this was for us encouragement, a renewal of faith in the value of our lives; but also, inseparably, it was challenge. The power of St Thérèse's life did not come merely from the fact that she entered Carmel, wore a Carmelite habit, but from the white-hot intensity with which she lived that life. Bishop Comiskey was referring to this when he said that the casket contained 'not just bones' but 'the remains of a burnt-out love for God'. The value, the power for good, of our life in Carmel, or outside it, depends on the love with which we live. Like Thérèse, we can only draw that love from its source in the Heart of Jesus. She saw that it was by being herself ever more closely united to Jesus that she would effectively draw others to Him. That is clearly our mission as Carmelites, and it was brought home to us anew very powerfully by the experience of Thérèse's visit.

But Thérèse's 'weapons' of prayer and sacrifice as expressions of love are not exclusive to Carmel. Like Thérèse herself, they are readily accessible to everyone. Thérèse's daily sacrifices were humble little acts of unselfishness and kindness, giving of herself to others with a smile or a helping hand, restraining the sharp reply or dismissive gesture. These 'little' things, united to Jesus' great sacrifice, were the stuff of her sanctity and the source of her wealth. She invites us to make them our own.

Indeed, was it not just such things that were so strongly in evidence during her stay among us, visible signs of the working of her spirit? Everywhere she went she generated a great good will, a readiness to help, an atmosphere of friendliness and joy. The time of her visit was for us all a kind of Tabor experience. Everyone felt it was good for us to be here. Her presence brought out the best in everyone, a revelation to us all of the latent good in ourselves and in all others who shared the experience with us. It was like a flash of lightning that lit up much that was there, shrouded in darkness. The light may have faded with the departure of the relics, but we must not forget that moment of light when we saw much that was for our comfort.

We saw people coming in their thousands; we saw their reverence, their prayerfulness, witnessing to genuine faith and devotion. We saw the generous commitment that went into organising the event, the concern and care for the invalids, the thought for the prisoners and the disadvantaged, the dedication and sensitivity of the Gardaí — the list is endless. St Thérèse was shown to have legions of friends in our country; and lovers of Thérèse must sooner or later be lovers of Jesus, for she always points beyond herself to Him — witness the numbers availing of the Sacrament of Reconciliation. We must not forget these things as we continue on 'dark ways of faith'. We are not walking alone with the Lord, but all those thousands of people are walking with us, bolstering up our wavering faith. 'Jesus is enough' — undoubtedly, yes, but it is good nonetheless, and very good, to know of all that great company marching with us. We can put heart into one another. Praying now, here in our choir in Carmel, we remember all those people who crowded in to pray with us at the 'time of the relics' and we know that they are out there still praying with us, for us, as we for them. The Communion of Saints has taken on a new flesh-and-blood reality for us.

There was a radiation from the reliquary, as Bishop Comiskey said. We were all aware of it. 'But,' he said, pointing to the tabernacle, 'a far greater radiation from there!' Perhaps we are less aware of that because it is there all the time. We were sensitised, tuned in to the radiation from the reliquary by the sense of occasion. St Thérèse would not have us feel bereft at the departure of her relics and overlook the treasure of the real Presence we have always in our midst. If we tune in to that Presence, we will surely find ourselves in communion with Thérèse also, as indeed with the whole host of Heaven. A heightened awareness of that abiding Presence in our midst would be a wonderful legacy of her visit.

For the apostles, Tabor was a preparation for Calvary. St Thérèse set a high value on the cross for herself, and evidently still does so for her friends. It is remarkable that a significant number of our friends who were very involved with the visit of the relics have since met with crosses of various kinds — the death of loved ones, serious illness for themselves or for those nearest and dearest to them. I know that St Thérèse has been with them all the way, obtaining for them strength, comfort and peace. For Thérèse herself, everything that came to her from the hand of God was the gift of His love, an opportunity to respond to love, to grow in love.

The exciting days of her visit to us have given place to the humdrum ordinariness of our daily lives, but it is precisely there that Thérèse would have us find the Lord. If we continue to listen to her, she will help us to love what she loved and live as she taught us. We will come to understand with her the wonderful truth that 'everything is grace'.

Sister Immaculata ODC
Hampton Carmel, Grace Park Road, Dublin

I had read a lot about the fashions and frivolity of Paris. These were in evidence in every street, but the churches stood noticeably apart from these scenes. A man would forget the outside noise and bustle as soon as he entered one of these churches. His manner would change, he would behave with dignity and reverence as he passed someone kneeling before the image of the Virgin. The feeling I had then has since been growing on me, that all this kneeling and prayer could not be mere superstition; the devout souls kneeling before the Virgin could not be worshipping mere marble. They were fired with genuine devotion and they worshipped not stone, but the divinity of which it was symbolic. I have an impression that I felt then that by this worship they were not detracting from, but increasing, the glory of God.

FROM THE AUTOBIOGRAPHY OF MAHATMA GANDHI

Introduction

On the evening of 10 September 2001, just fourteen hours before history ruptured and a new and terrifying reality dawned in both the United States and the wider world, I was in Loretto, Pennsylvania, visiting the Carmelite Monastery of St Thérèse of Lisieux. It was my second visit to this monastery, built as an exact replica of the Carmel convent in Lisieux, France. It was there, on 1 November 1999, I first encountered the dome-covered reliquary of the Little Flower and discovered that Thérèse of Lisieux was 'on tour' across the globe.

On that date in 1999 I had journeyed to see my nearest sibling, Deirdre, a Sister of Mercy, who was a visiting professor at Mount Aloysius College, Cresson, Pennsylvania. In the early evening, as we sat down to dinner, Deirdre mentioned in passing that the relics of St Thérèse had arrived that afternoon in the neighbouring town of Loretto, just a few miles away.

Since 1974–75 I have had an on-off interest in St Thérèse. Finding myself in the rare and happy coincidence of visiting the same out-of-the-way neighbourhood as one of my two favourite saints (St Francis of Assisi being the other), I asked if we could drive to Loretto following our meal.

Together with Sr Charlene Kelly, we arrived at the Carmel monastery to discover a large, good-humoured crowd, organised in two queues, stretching several hundred yards in opposite directions. We joined one and slowly made our way inside the chapel and up to the beautiful reliquary that was to become so familiar in Ireland less than two years later.

As in Ireland, I was immediately struck by the quiet and prayerful dignity that permeated the atmosphere of the occasion. I was also very taken by a joyful radiance that seemed to emanate from the Carmelite Sisters, who, for this special occasion, were making a rare public appearance.

Finding myself back in the neighbourhood to give the opening convocation address at Mount Aloysius College on Monday, 10 September 2001, I contacted the prioress, Mother John of the Cross, who invited me to visit the monastery that same evening to speak to the Sisters about the visit to Ireland of the relics of St Thérèse and some of the stories I had collected. In a very real sense, my first encounter with the reliquary at the Loretto Carmel was the seed of this book and the beginning of a journey that has rekindled my respect for Thérèse of Lisieux and her quest for truth.

The idea for the book gradually dawned as I visited several venues during the reliquary's eighty-day visit to Ireland. On Easter Sunday, 15 April 2001, the day of its arrival, I drove to Enniscorthy, Co. Wexford, with my friend John Coyle, to pay respects and, in a very real sense, to welcome Thérèse to Ireland. I immediately recognised the same prayerful reverence around the reliquary that I had experienced in Loretto, Pennsylvania, in 1999.

It was clear that something very deep was stirred by the visit of the reliquary of St Thérèse. Unquestionably it highlighted the fact that, despite the secularisation of Irish society, there still remained a deep well of spirituality that had sustained Irish people through many harsh periods of their history. Initially, organisers were tantalising the public with advance posters: one claimed that an unnamed 'she' would draw bigger crowds than rock legends U2 drew to Slane; another boasted that 'she' was more popular than pop star Madonna. When eventually it was revealed that 'she' was in fact a box of old bones of a young nineteenth-century saint, the boast seemed to be the work of lunatics. When they informed the media that upwards of one million people were expected to visit the reliquary, it sounded so outrageous that many, including some in the hierarchy, wondered if the organisers had lost their reason.

From the moment the reliquary arrived, however, endless crowds formed queues that snaked out of convents and cathedral grounds for a quarter of a mile and more. They included devotees, doubters, the curious and even cynics. They shuffled forward, sometimes in pouring rain and cold winds, with good humour and kindness. Large numbers of the travelling community were particularly visible everywhere she went. They filed in lines of faith and fervour, often for hours, to stand before the sacred reliquary of Thérèse for a few brief seconds.

To almost all, touch was important. It was an attempt, perhaps, to reach out and experience the presence of one so close to God. Many came because of a personal friendship with the Little Flower of Lisieux — a devotion often cultivated in the garden of their childhood by a mother's faith that left a lasting impression in their hearts and minds. They came to talk to Thérèse about loved ones who

were sick and in need of healing. They came to unburden worries
and woes, to seek grace and insight to enable them to continue the
challenge of living.

At St Eugene's Cathedral, Derry, for example, on 31 July 2001, I
spoke to the widow of a Bloody Sunday victim. She is a woman of
immense dignity and strength. Her simple devotion to the Little
Flower, she said, was something that had helped her cope with the
loss of a young husband and the momentous responsibilities of
raising sons and daughters during the darkest days of the 'Troubles'.

A few cynics poured scorn on the visit of the reliquary. To the
sceptical, the unbelieving and the indifferent it was utter nonsense,
a source of bemusement and ridicule. For some, too, it was a sacri-
lege and a scandal. Indeed, there were places where the reliquary,
on advice from the RUC, quietly took long diversions in order not to
cause offence to some non-Catholic denominations in Northern
Ireland. For some, the idea of carting around a box (albeit a
beautifully carved and decorated box) holding a few odd bones,
taken from the remains of a young woman who died in 1897, was
ridiculous — a sure sign of regression, of an attempt to clip the claws
of the Celtic Tiger, to reinvent an Ireland that they had hoped was
drawing its last breath. Some saw it as a last-gasp attempt by a
wounded Catholic Church to give itself the kiss of life, in the hope
of resuscitating the good old days when bishops and priests were
feudal lords in their dioceses and parishes.

However, from the moment the reliquary arrived on Irish soil it
was clear that the outpouring of affection would exceed even the
expectations of the organisers. The phenomenon was repeated
across the island, as tens of thousands of citizens arrived at all hours
of the day and night to pay their quiet respects. What impressed me

most was the lack of triumphalism. There were no bishop band-wagons and no clerical clowning. This was something that seemed to confuse and fascinate religious professionals as much as the press.

The Bishop of Derry, Seamus Hegarty, openly admitted he was overwhelmed by the outpouring of reverence and devotion, and said he was aware of seven or eight Protestants who had also come to visit the reliquary at St Eugene's Cathedral. 'This is not ecclesiastical gymnastics,' he told me. 'People are genuinely very moved.' Those privileged to stand by the reliquary spoke to him of a most intense experience. 'They have witnessed people approach with joy, worry, hurt and disillusionment.' He spoke of a tremendous grace of repentance that so many people received. 'Five or six priests are constantly hearing Confessions. It is an inexplicable working of grace.'

'Thérèse's mission,' Bishop Hegarty said, 'is going to have a very important significance in the Church. It marks the beginning of a new epoch. It is not without significance the Pope named her a Doctor of the Church — an honour given to very few.'

By the time Thérèse's relics left Ireland, it was estimated that somewhere in the region of two and a half to three million people, predominantly Catholic, had venerated them. I was certain that, given the volume of people who visited the reliquary, many, if willing, would have stories to tell of their encounter with a saint who prophesied that she would spend her Heaven doing good and would let fall upon the Earth a shower of roses.

This book is testimony to many of those stories. I am indebted to all who generously took the time to share their experiences so that a unique repository of witness statements from Thérèse's visit to

Ireland might be published. In a very real sense, it is a unique snapshot of how a diverse group of people encountered Thérèse of Lisieux's journey through Ireland. While specific to Ireland, their encounter is, I believe, a universal experience.

There is much here that will be a source of encouragement and edification to lovers of Thérèse. There are perspectives and opinions expressed with which some will disagree. I choose, however, to be respectful of the wide cross-section of opinion expressed. On reading *Story of a Soul*, it is clear that Thérèse was often misunderstood and that even choices she made as part of her Little Way were unjustly misinterpreted. Despite this, Thérèse's own sense of justice and charity moved her to search for the silver lining. I have no doubt that Thérèse respects the struggle for truth that is at the core of each and every contribution published.

Not all contributions are complimentary. Many are very witty and engaging. An important series of contributions are thoughtful reflections on the meaning of Thérèse's message and its relevance to a wounded Irish Church. The majority of testimonies, however, introduce the reader to encounters with the young saint that range from the miraculous to the mundane. They are published here as the genuine experiences of some Irish people. Neither my publisher nor I consider ourselves competent to adjudicate on the mysterious nature of many of the testimonies published. We do believe, however, that they are sincere accounts and, as such, are worthy of consideration.

Not all contributions could be included, but all contributions will be deposited in a Carmelite archive, probably in Lisieux. I hope that those published in this modest volume will be a source of comfort and encouragement to all who are struggling with faith and with life's meaning. I have no doubt that the testimonies published are but a tiny fraction of many stories that are yet untold. Should readers wish to contribute further testimonies, they are invited to do so by writing to the address below.

The title of the book is the contribution of my youngest daughter Emma, aged eight. One evening, while I was working on the book, she climbed the stairs to my attic office and presented me with two drawings she had made for me. Both depicted several red roses, across which she had written the name of St Thérèse and the title 'A Gift of Roses'. Many of the testimonies in this book are, indeed, just that.

❧

Like many Catholics the world over, I had my first introduction to St Thérèse, the Little Flower, through my mother. I recall from my childhood a simple prayer she repeated three times at the end of the family rosary:

Little Flower, in this hour, show thy power.

I am not quite sure where Thérèse ranked in the hierarchy of favourite saints, but she certainly did not hold the number-one spot in the simple faith that dwelt in my mother's heart. That was reserved for the sixteenth-century black Dominican friar, St Martin de Porres, from Lima, Peru. My mother loved the *St Martin Magazine*, and on many occasions I recall her reading stories from the publication after I returned home from school.

I first became aware of Thérèse's title 'Patroness of the Missions' on her feast day, 1 October 1973. I was in my first year of studying for the missionary priesthood at St Patrick's College, Buchlyvie,

Scotland. We were given the day off from studies, so she immediately made a favourable impact.

It was not, however, until the following academic year, 1974–75,
that I was introduced to Thérèse in a deeper sense. By then I had
moved to St Patrick's Missionary College, Kiltegan, Co. Wicklow, to
participate in what was called a spiritual year. It was a very privileged year during which we had the opportunity to study the
Scriptures, along with some introductory philosophy and theology.
My favourite teaching professor was Father Paddy Kelly.

Father Kelly spoke with gentle passion and genuine conviction
that was born from a life of deep prayer and meditation. Almost
thirty years later, I recall the experience of listening to this priest with
a sense of profound gratitude. When he spoke of Thérèse, something resonated in my spirit.

Father Paddy talked of Thérèse's struggle with her own human
limitations. Like her, I struggled with my studies and with the discipline imposed during what was a highly regimented and structured
year. He spoke of Thérèse's ordinariness and her desire to do
ordinary things in an extraordinary way. He spoke of her heart for
all humanity, despite the fact that her most profound years were
spent within the confines of the Carmelite enclosure in Lisieux.
Above all, he spoke of her discovery of a fresh and innovative way
of living the simple and uncomplicated Gospel commandment of
loving God and one's neighbour as oneself. He spoke of Thérèse's
uncomplicated and childlike response to the love of a merciful God
whose spirit dwells deep in our hearts and far less in our heads.

As the summer of 1975 approached, the thought of visiting
Lisieux became a compelling idea. I discussed the possibility with
my best friend, Shaunie McLaughlin, with whom I had hitchhiked

around Ireland in 1972. Shaunie and I were, in the literal sense, soulmates. We agreed to hike through Normandy, our two main objectives being Lisieux and the famous Benedictine Abbey of Mont Saint-Michel.

In August 1975 we left Derry for Rosslare and took the ferry to Le Havre. From there we thumbed our way to Lisieux via Caen, where we visited the tomb of William the Conqueror in the Cathedral of St Etienne. When we arrived in Lisieux, one of the first people we met was a most kind and gentle priest, Monsignor Georges Durand, with whom we formed an immediate friendship. He arranged for us to stay at the *Foyer de St Thérèse*.

After three days we moved on to Mont Saint-Michel and spent our first night in a hostel close to the top of the conical island crowned by the famous monastery. I was surprised, the following morning, when Shaunie said he would like to return to Lisieux and spend the rest of our holiday there. I, of course, was delighted, and we departed immediately.

I cherish the photographs from that holiday with my best friend. I still retain the copy of Thérèse's autobiography I purchased that year. The paper has browned with age and the front cover is hanging by a thread from being packed in rucksacks and suitcases.

The opportunity to visit all the places in Lisieux mentioned in *Story of a Soul* was a delight. Several times we crisscrossed Lisieux, exploring the places associated with the young saint: the Carmel chapel and the hall of relics; the Cathedral of St Pierre, where she made her First Confession; *Les Buissonnets*, the Martin family home after they moved from Alençon following the death of Mrs Martin in 1877; the municipal cemetery where, in 1897, Thérèse was the first Carmelite buried outside of the Carmel enclosure, due to a new law; and the great Basilica of St Thérèse.

It was at the Basilica that my most memorable moment of that 1975 visit occurred. A life-sized marble statue of St Thérèse, clutching a crucifix and roses, stood to the side of an altar dedicated to the people of the USA. I recall a large vase of red roses placed at the base of the statue, before which was a small pew.

Shaunie knelt before the statue. He was twenty and I was nineteen. He was a talented professional footballer who had spent time with Leicester City and Hibernians of Edinburgh. He was, at that time, playing for the League of Ireland team Dundalk. He was popular in Derry, had a good education, a good job and a bright future. Something, however, happened as he knelt before the statue. He remained kneeling for at least thirty minutes. I sat in the background, waiting.

When he rose he looked at me and said, 'I don't know what happened to me. I felt as though time stopped.' He searched for an adequate explanation and then said, 'It was a timeless experience.' There was a serenity about him that I could see reflected in his eyes. We never discussed it further, but I knew that something profound had occurred during those precious minutes before the statue of St Thérèse, and I felt glad that my best friend had followed his instincts and returned to Lisieux to experience whatever it was.

A year later, almost to the day, Shaunie was dead, killed in a multiple automobile accident on 22 August 1976. This year, 2001, marked the twenty-fifth anniversary of his death. Despite the passage of time, I still feel his loss.

After that pilgrimage, my interest in Thérèse of Lisieux somewhat wavered. I left the seminary at the end of 1975 due to my father's illness. I worked in Derry for a couple of years in an assortment of jobs before returning to college, where I qualified as a youth and community worker and later did Third World Studies at the Holy Ghost Missionary College, Kimmage, Dublin. I often talked about Thérèse's sense of humanity; but, apart from that, I was somewhat lukewarm and getting colder. When my wife Margaret gave birth to our first daughter in 1987, however, we decided to name her Thérèse. After that the light flickered but weakly.

Then, in 1991, two encounters occurred which caused me to rediscover Thérèse in a new way. The first was my discovery that the great American Catholic activist and social radical, Dorothy Day, had written a biography about the saint that she simply called *Thérèse*. I had always been an admirer of Dorothy Day, co-founder of the Catholic Worker Movement that provided shelter for America's homeless. The Movement also sought to inform American public opinion regarding the Gospel perspective on divisive subjects such as the black civil rights movement, Vietnam and US foreign policy throughout the world. Long before many of us knew where Nicaragua was located or even how to spell it, Day was supporting the struggle of Augusto Sandino against what she saw as American imperialism in Central America.

The second encounter involved a conversation with the Anglican Primate of Southern Africa and Nobel Laureate, Archbishop Desmond Tutu, at Louisburgh, Co. Mayo, on the morning of 6 April 1991. He had come to lead the annual AFrI Great 'Famine' Walk. With colleagues and friends from AFrI, we attended the Archbishop's Mass at the Old Head Hotel, Louisburgh, and then, while awaiting our call to breakfast, engaged him in conversation around a large log fire. I asked him who his favourite saints were and he answered, 'Mary Magdalene, St Francis of Assisi and the Little Flower.' He then told us that he and his wife Leah had named their eldest daughter, Theresa Thandeka, after the saint.

My friendship with Desmond Tutu began in 1982 when, with AFrI colleagues, we organised a three-day conference on World Peace and Poverty to celebrate the eight hundredth anniversary of the birth of St Francis of Assisi. I had grown to love and respect this gentle but fearless opponent of apartheid, whom Nelson Mandela was to call 'Pastor of the Nation'. The fact that he spoke with such tender affection about Thérèse of Lisieux re-ignited my youthful interest.

I recall those youthful days with amazement now. While not a zealot, I was motivated with an idealism that filled me with a desire to convert the planet to Christianity, and specifically to Roman Catholicism. Almost thirty years later, my conviction has dramatically changed. Far from wishing to convert the world to Catholicism, I have come to the belief that in this culturally rich and diverse world there are many pathways to God. They have, however, a common denominator: a life motivated by a spirit of compassion, generosity and justice. I do not believe we will be judged on the membership badge of one particular faith or another, but on the quality of our relationships to one another. Jesus told His disciples that the world would recognise them as His followers if they had love for one another. The love that Jesus spoke of is a universal gift of God. It is not something exclusive to Catholicism or to Christianity. It is a love, for example, that someone like the gentle Hindu prophet Mahatma Gandhi understood far more clearly than many Christians he encountered in India and throughout the British Empire.

I have come to reject the concept of a God who apparently sits, like Scrooge, with grubby fingers protruding out of fingerless gloves, tabulating and weighing every thought and prayer. I reject the concept of a fundamentalist God who delights in His followers rigidly adhering to man-made rules and ordinances, and who is so restrictive and joyless He wishes the whole world to be converted to small-minded pettiness. I reject the concept of a God who permits His followers to commit mass murder in His name and who bestows holy martyrdom on those who do it. I reject the concept of an exclusively Roman Catholic God as much as I reject the concept of an exclusively Islamic, Jewish, Christian, Buddhist or Hindu God.

While Thérèse of Lisieux's life was rooted in the Scriptures, it might be said that St John's Gospel was her favourite, for it was here she principally discovered her vocation. Her autobiography seems to climax around the insights she obtained from John's Gospel concerning the new commandment Jesus gave to his disciples at the end of the Last Supper:

> A new commandment I give you, that you love one another: that as I have loved you, you also love one another. By this will all people know that you are my disciples, if you have love for one another. (John 13:34)

Therein lies the essence of Thérèse of Lisieux. Her vocation was to be love in the heart of the Church. While she was never to venture outside the confines of the Lisieux Carmel, her heart pulsated with a sense of all humanity.

Her love was not perfect, and she was, like all human beings, limited by the cultural heritage of her time and place. Some of the language in her autobiography, like the use of the words 'savage' and 'infidels' when describing non-Christian indigenous people in Asia, Africa and the Americas, is grating.

Thérèse's personality was shaped by an overprotective family upbringing heavily influenced by her French Roman Catholic faith, which still retained the odour of Jansenism's frigidity and inhibitions. As such, Thérèse Martin presents, particularly in the earlier part of her autobiography, the image of a young female with many limitations. It would be easy to dislike the oversensitive, sometimes obstinate and mollycoddled little girl that she was. There were those who clearly disliked her. She tells us in her auto-biography that their housemaid, Victoire, whom she frequently annoyed, often called her 'a little brat'.

But there is also something charmingly refreshing about her fearless exposé of her many faults and shortcomings. For example, in Chapter IV of *Story of a Soul* she recalls a retreat at the Benedictine Abbey, Lisieux, in preparation for her first Holy Communion which she made there on 8 May 1884:

> In the morning, I found it very nice to see all the students getting up so early and doing the same as they; but I was not yet accustomed to taking care of myself. Marie was not there to comb and curl my hair, and so I was obliged to go and timidly offer my comb to the mistress in charge of the dressing rooms. She laughed at seeing a big girl of eleven not knowing how to take care of herself, and still she combed my hair but not as gently as Marie.

There is no doubt that Thérèse was doted upon, shielded and overprotected, especially after the death of her mother when she was just four and a half. When one realises that she was the youngest of nine children and that her four youngest siblings had died in infancy or as toddlers, one begins to understand the great care and attention lavished upon her.

It is important to kee

born a saint. It is the int

and her many shortcomin

transforms her autobiogra

discovered her vocation to be

and ultimately humanity. She

compassionate, forgiving and a

tional love. Near the end of her life

> I am a very little soul and ... I can ... ... .e things ...
> the Lord is so good to me that it is ... .ie for me to fear
> Him.

Her Little Way of trust and confidence is the backbone of her fearlessness in this great God of goodness. Her way is the essence of simplicity — a Little Way available to all little souls like her. At heart, it is a way of living in the present, of harnessing the opportunities of our humdrum lives — especially the suffering of the sick and infirm — and of injecting them with meaning and purpose.

While Thérèse's Little Way may be simple, it is not, however, easy. It is challenging to the core and, like her own epic struggle, will lead us to the front line in the battle against all manifestations of human selfishness. Thérèse's heart for all humanity leads us to embrace the politics of compassion, and to aspire towards a new world order where the love of God and one's neighbour motivates us to work for a world filled with justice and gentleness — a world where all human beings, irrespective of their culture, ethnicity, gender, and ideological or religious beliefs, must learn to live and let live.

For Thérèse, there was no discontinuity between life and death. At the moment her human life expired, her spirit was released from the envelope of its limitations and made a seamless passage to Life with

etness and roses. Doubts threatened to
aith during moments of grave suffering and

se's struggle with faith, in the final months of her young
, is a source of consolation to many who struggle with belief. It is
one of the reasons why I, in a very real sense, have 'rediscovered'
her in recent years. I share her 'dark night of the soul'. There is
nothing within me that satisfies me that God actually exists. There is
no warm glow. No Damascus thunderbolt. No voices from heaven
or echoes in my soul. No joyous heartbeat to satisfy my hunger for
Truth. The nearest I come to an encounter with God is in my
contemplation of the universe. But still, I am left with the ultimate
question: Does God exist?

I, for one, cannot honestly answer such a profound question
with a simple 'Yes' or 'No'. For many, the question holds the key to
the essence of all meaning. For others, it is a question of torment.
For some, it is a question in which they have found deep serenity.
Many are indifferent to the question. Others don't have the time or
luxury to contemplate it, since their lives are ones of cruel existence
in a world of too much poverty, hunger, disease and pain.

Is it possible that all existence is nothing more than the conse-
quence of an ancient cosmic 'Big Bang'? Is human existence, in
particular, nothing more than the result of complex chemical
improbabilities that accidentally evolved following that initial
cosmic spark?

In her autobiography, St Thérèse recalls occasional Sunday
evenings in her childhood when, following visits to her uncle Isidore
Guérin's home in Lisieux, she would return home to *Les Buissonnets*
with her father. She writes:

When we were on the way home, I would gaze upon the stars that were twinkling ever so peacefully in the skies and the sight carried me away. There was especially one cluster of golden pearls that attracted my attention and gave me great joy because they were in the form of a 'T'. I pointed them out to Papa and told him my name was written in heaven. Then desiring to look no longer upon this dull earth, I asked him to guide my steps; and not looking where I placed my feet I threw back my head, giving myself over completely to the contemplation of the star-studded firmament!

Against a background of black velvet, Thérèse was drawn to the dazzling spectacle of the constellation of Orion, which dominates the northern hemisphere in winter. Her young eyes beheld three slanted stars — popularly referred to as Orion's belt — and other celestial objects that, to a lively imagination, formed the letter 'T'.

There is something charming in Thérèse's childish innocence, as revealed by this incident. The fact that she chose to recall it in the months leading up to her death also reveals that her faith had matured beyond the symbolism of a star pattern. As she fast approached the final frontier between life and death (at a time, it must be remembered, when crushing doubts about the very existence of God echoed in the fabric of her soul), Thérèse's heart profoundly understood a greater truth. If God existed, then not only was she part of a delightful star pattern in the constellation of Orion, she was part of the very essence of an infinite universe, which was itself a reflection of the God of Infinity who loved her and whom she loved.

Ever since I was a child, my eyes too have gazed at the night sky in wonderment. While I never found my name written amongst the stars, the breathtaking beauty and dimensions of the cosmos have caused the lungs of my spirit to expand with the deep breath of hope.

We now know that our planet, sun and Milky Way galaxy are not the centre of the universe. Indeed, we are but a tiny, insignificant speck in an unfathomable cosmic ocean. For every one of the few thousand stars we can see in our galaxy with the naked eye, there are fifty million we can't; and there are at least as many galaxies in the universe as there are stars in the Milky Way. The dimensions are both staggering and confounding.

On Good Friday 2001, while a small group of Irish people gathered in Lisieux to collect the sacred relics of St Thérèse for their eighty-day pilgrimage to Ireland, I visited the Rose Center for Earth and Space at the American Museum of Natural History on Central Park West, New York. A space show, *Passport to the Universe*, narrated by Tom Hanks, had been highly recommended by a friend, and I was determined to see it before my return flight to Dublin that evening. I had no idea of the impact it would have on me. I can only describe my feelings by the end of the show as the nearest I have ever come to a truly religious experience.

Through advanced digital technology and a three-dimensional projection system, the audience is taken on a cosmic journey from Earth, beyond our solar system and galaxy, to the farthest reaches of the observable universe. If the 'Big Bang' was, in fact, the beginning of time, astronomers now estimate that its impact has, so far, travelled thirteen billion light years in every direction. Part of the experience includes a cosmic pathway along a 360-foot spiral walkway that chronicles the thirteen-billion-year evolution of the universe. Visitors are informed that all of recorded human history amounts to no more than the width of a human hair at the end of the 360-foot ramp.

More mind-boggling is the possibility that our observable universe may itself be a tiny island in an as yet undiscovered universe.

In such a scenario the so-called 'Big Bang' may, in relative terms, have registered only as the pop of an exploding champagne cork on the edge of a yet unknown and unexplored cosmic frontier.

My flight back to Ireland was filled with thoughts of such magnitude, and the question of the existence of God felt very real. As the Aer Lingus flight touched down at Dublin Airport in the early hours of Easter Saturday morning, my sensitivity to the Gospel account of Christ's resurrection was heightened. I realised profoundly that belief is a choice. And, like Thérèse of Lisieux in the final months of her life, I understood that, for some, belief in an all-powerful and loving Creator is, quite literally, an act of blind faith when our souls are devoid of light and seem filled by an arid landscape.

It felt good to be back in that little patch of the planet I call home: not least to see my family, but also because our eldest daughter Thérèse would, by happy coincidence, later that day board Irish Ferries' *MV Normandy* — the ship that would carry to Rosslare the sacred relics of the saint after whom she was named. The next day, the first Easter Sunday of the third millennium, Thérèse of Lisieux, 'the greatest saint of modern times,' would begin an epic journey through Ireland — a quiet journey of breathtaking and historic proportions.

Don Mullan
P.O. Box 5244, Dublin 12, Ireland
1 November 2001 (All Saints' Day)

'... it is only love that makes us acceptable to God....'
Thérèse of Lisieux

Moments Never to be Forgotten

Interview with Father J. Linus Ryan O.Carm.
National Co-ordinator, St Thérèse's Relics' Irish Visit

Don Mullan: Where did your devotion to St Thérèse begin?

Father Linus Ryan: I was born a few years after St Thérèse's canonisation, at a time when almost every Catholic home in Ireland was full of St Thérèse. She was so popular — the saint carrying the bunch of roses, who loved flowers. I grew up with that image in the background; but I would have to truthfully say that, as a young boy, she wouldn't have impinged very much on my life. I would have been more interested in football, sport and what I was reading.

I joined the Carmelite Order after my Leaving Cert, went to the novitiate in Kinsale and began to read her autobiography. I saw a whole new dimension to Thérèse — that she was a serious person wanting to influence the quality of my life for the better. My relationship, I think, began there.

No matter what spiritual reading I did, I allocated a certain portion of each day to Thérèse — normally her autobiography — and I felt that, as I went about my priestly work, words came easily to me in dealing with other souls in the confessional and elsewhere. I found various parallels in Thérèse's life to the difficulties a penitent might be experiencing at any particular time. People were very often consoled to know that St Thérèse had similar problems. She had to fight the lower side of human nature, which we all have to fight — selfishness, self-centredness, pride, vanity, all those things that are part of our every day, rearing their heads at virtually every point of our existence. She is tremendously important to people and certainly has been tremendously important to me.

Thérèse constantly makes each of us realise how valuable we are, that each of us is a unique creation in the sight of God, that each of us has been given a certain work to do. She dignified the suffering of people in wheelchairs, people who were confined to bed, people who were paralysed, people who feel useless and, in a sense, burdens on society. She restored the sense of dignity to everybody by making them realise just how much, in all that terrible suffering and frustration, they could contribute to the mystical Body of Christ and to the salvation and sanctification of souls.

DM: Why do you think that non-Catholics like Archbishop Desmond Tutu, and even non-Christians, would find an attraction to Thérèse?

FR RYAN: Everybody loves a lover. Everybody loves an achiever. Everybody loves somebody who gives their heart's blood for an ideal while not looking for a spot in the sunshine. She was quite prepared to go to hell if in hell she could love God. The depth of that type of love.... Nobody except the divine Master has ever uttered language of love before like Thérèse has.

She wants to love God as he has never been loved before, and she doesn't want anybody to know about it in case she is attracting attention to herself. In other words, she is the very antithesis of the things we aspire to: the vainglory, the spot in the sun, the glamour of being in the headlines, being in the newspapers, being in the photographs. She is a marvellous humanitarian by any standards. In a strange way, too, she identifies with people of no faith: at the end, if she were to discover there was no heaven, she would have no regrets about pursuing the path and paying the price she did.

She was tempted to doubt. From the time she began to haemorrhage, she experienced a dark night of terrible temptations against faith. But she never gave in. She endured the terrible sense of hopelessness that suicidal people endure but never gave in. That's why she is such a model of faith. She continued to believe, to hope against hope and believe against belief. Imaginary voices mocked her, saying, 'You dream in vain, you are approaching the night of complete nothingness.' She had to battle against that for the last eighteen months of her life.

DM: Where did your confidence come from? Many people felt you were wide of the mark, and yet you were proven to be modest in your predictions.

FR RYAN: My particular job as national co-ordinator gave me a perspective that probably nobody else shared in the country. I had to read the reports of all the countries that had gone before us, and I suddenly saw that there was a common denominator — there were four or five points that were common to them all. One of the things that all the co-ordinators say is, 'Think big, and it will be even bigger than you think.' Another was, 'Be ready for the Confessions; there will be enormous numbers, and the quality will be high.'

There was a pattern of goodness, and a pattern of achievement, that was there for every country. Wherever she was going, she was bringing a certain sense of well-being, a certain peace, a certain charity; but, above all, she was focusing on the Sacrament of Penance and Reconciliation, which doesn't surprise me. When you think about it, she has an awful lot to say about the mercy of God. Her Act of Oblation is to the merciful love of God. To me it's no surprise that she is focused on the Sacrament of Reconciliation, because that's where the mercy of God is dispensed in this life in a very special way.

The numbers everywhere had exceeded all their estimates. If this was true, particularly for the very materialist United States, it had to be true for here. I stuck with a certain optimism that was based, not on a hunch, but on certain observations of the reports.

Another thing was that in a lot of countries there was too much pontificating, and people were kept away for long periods from the reliquary; it was cordoned off with ceremonial rope, and you could have long liturgies going on for a good deal of the time. People would be in line outside, feeling very frustrated that they couldn't come and venerate the relics. From early on, we made it very clear that this was going to be people-centred, and that the primary concern of each venue would be to facilitate large numbers coming to visit the reliquary; that they would have facilities for the sick and invalids, and that liturgies would be reduced to a minimum in order to focus on the veneration of the relics.

If there is anything unique that Ireland contributed to the general veneration of the relics, it is the all-night vigils. That facilitated working people. They didn't have to get off work. It meant that whole families could come together. It wasn't unusual to see a whole family — father, mother and children — at eleven o'clock, or midnight, all come in together. There was no pressure; whatever time they arrived, the church was open to greet them.

DM: When and why did you decide to host the relics?

FR RYAN: We applied to host the relics in 1997, the centenary year of her death, but the correspondence was lost. We applied again in 1999. We thought it would go well here, since there was a good core of Thérèse devotion, and that is something I noticed as I went around in the Thérèsemobile: I found in a lot of the country towns you had little altars in the windows of homes. What struck me was the number of pictures of Thérèse that were obviously old pictures. They certainly would have gone back to the time of her canonisation, and maybe even before it. I was deducing that there was an awful solid devotion to Thérèse in the homes of Ireland.

There are about eight members in the Thérèsian Trust, which is centred up in Hampton Carmel in the old novitiate. We thought that we might apply again, so this time they asked me to try and deal on a personal basis, because I was well known in Lisieux, as I had been running the Irish National Pilgrimage to Lisieux for over thirty years. I did, and was received extremely well, but they wouldn't say yes until they had a formal invitation from the Irish Bishops' Conference, to make sure the visit had full episcopal approval.

I asked Bishop Comiskey if he would bring up the question of permission at the next meeting of bishops, and he said he would. Bishop Brendan is a friend, and I had brought him to Lisieux a few times on the National Pilgrimage. For a long time he had no particular devotion to Thérèse; he just came to oblige me. He generally spent the four or five days in Lisieux reading. He would, of course, be available for Mass and events associated with the pilgrimage, but otherwise he scampered to his room. After a while he began to read a bit about Thérèse, and she nabbed him — that's the only word I can use. He became completely absorbed with Thérèse and she with him; it's as simple as that.

He became a tremendous chairperson of the organising committee. He got the backing of the bishops. Once their invitation went through, Lisieux was anxious to deal with somebody on the ground whom they knew. Fortunately I was very well known to them, so that's how I fell into the co-ordinator's position.

The acceptance for Ireland came through by fax on St Patrick's Day 1999. Our plan was to go to all the Carmelite monasteries and all the diocesan cathedrals. In that sense we were satisfying the Carmelites — of which Thérèse was a member — and by going to every diocese there was an element of inclusiveness, so no part of the country could feel hard done by.

It worked extremely well. It proved to be a very dynamic thing and a very good way to do it. It eliminated rivalry and the human side that can come to the fore in all these things, and every diocese felt it had its day. In one sense it was a master stroke; in another sense it was a Thérèse stroke. She inspired us from the beginning.

There was a lot of hard work, and I had a very good team — particularly Pat Sweeney and Fathers Eugene McCaffrey OCD, Des Flanagan O.Carm., Philip Brennan O.Carm. and Christopher O'Donnell O.Carm. I was given the opportunity by my Provincial to work full-time, and I was given office space by the prior of my community here in Terenure College, who gave us three rooms over two years. It was hard work, but with the collaboration of many people we got a great programme together. We had the media almost totally on our side as the days went on. Some days you would almost feel you wouldn't want the phone to ring again, you would be so tired. I think I did six or seven live radio interviews in one day.

DM: Looking back over the eighty days, how do you feel?

FR RYAN: I have a feeling of great gratitude. When you saw queues hundreds of yards long, you felt very grateful that it was a success. I haven't the slightest doubt that the hand of God and the hand of Thérèse touched the hearts of people. There is no human explanation for the behaviour of the people that was so wonderful in so many ways.

There was a tremendous sense of satisfaction and gratitude. I could have done all this work and it could have been a failure.... God has blessed us. You felt very humble. I haven't the slightest doubt that the good Lord took over; that's the only way you can explain such a mass movement of our people, and such peace and serenity and such co-operation.

The budding cynics were silenced early on. Extraordinary, given the media's hostility to religion over such a long period — at the very least they were neutral, and in most cases very positive. It was a tremendous thing to get Joe Duffy's *Liveline* programme, Donncha Ó Dúlaing's *Fáilte Isteach* and Gerry Ryan of 2FM on our side; they are three national broadcasters who are touching the lives of people every day. And, again, I felt that Thérèse had a hand in all of that.

The 'box of old bones' thing picked up a certain amount of popular dissent in the very early stages, before the pilgrimage happened at all. I'd say some of the clergy probably were a bit cynical initially about it — but it grew and grew. We had no problem getting extra priests in at night to hear Confessions, right through the night. If nothing else happened during those eighty days, except the Confessions, I would still say that the hand of God was mightily there.

The number of times we were held up — hijacked almost.... It was tremendous to see hundreds of people in knots along the road, little altars carefully prepared, maybe a couple of people in wheelchairs, sick people in cars — they all waited. We had to stop. That was a feature that we hadn't anticipated. Initially we felt that, going from one place to the other, yes, we might stop in the market square of some town; maybe a few people might cluster around. But we needed the Guards to sort out the gridlock — and not just with Dublin. Without them, we would have had tremendous traffic problems everywhere. We had outriders for the entire eighty days, including the RUC.

The Lord had it all prepared, and I think something has happened; I think that Church life in Ireland will never be the same again. It has left a mark; it wasn't just an eighty-day wonder. The hand of God and the hand of Thérèse have been firmly placed on the Irish Church. It's up to others, those in pastoral care for souls, to discern fully where we must go after this. There is a message, of course, for all of us.

DM: What do you think that message might be?

FR RYAN: I honestly don't know, but it would seem to me that our approach to religion was over-cerebral, since Vatican II. The saints and the culture of the saints have a very special place in our lives, and you only had to see the Divine approbation to think seriously about it: if God is producing miracles through the saints, He obviously has an interest in the cult of the saint.

The Second Vatican Council was right to re-focus on the centrality of the Eucharistic Mystery and on the centrality of God and the Trinity. These Councils, in one way or another, brought the Church back to the centre of its existence. Like all things, the Church gets frayed at the edges: it can lose focus, the accidental in life may begin to take a little bit of precedence over the substantial, so there is a need to take care and have a fresh look. The sensible side of religion seemed to have been frowned on, and I think people were upset.

But, you see, it's easy for theologians, people who are *au fait* with Church documents, to see the nuances and see the direction in which the Church is pointing and the things it's trying to say. To filter that down to people in the street, who have been weaned on years of a particular type of devotion, is not an easy thing, and I think a lot of people are a bit upset. Things that have happened since Vatican II have upset a lot of people. I'm not for a second criticising Vatican II, but it is the way people handled it.

DM: Are there any abiding memories you have of your eighty days around Ireland in the Thérèsemobile?

FR RYAN: Yes. One would be the number of sick and the number of wheelchairs. I think virtually anybody who wasn't totally bedridden managed to get out to a local venue. You marvel at the amount of suffering there is, and you marvel at their patience and faith. We made it a priority at all the venues to have special facilities for the sick. I have a very strong memory of the number of sick people who came in hope to Thérèse and, I'm sure, received a special embrace from her — maybe not exactly what they were hoping for, but certainly she would have sent nobody away empty-handed.

It wasn't easy to ferry people to some of the venues. You saw all these specially adapted buses for wheelchair users, and it was a tremendously consoling sight; and I think it had a major impact on people in the whole of their health. There are some terrible sufferings, some terrible physical handicaps — particularly when you see young children — that get to the heart of every person. There were many young children on those wheelchairs. We were also very moved to come around a bend in the road and find maybe twenty-five to thirty wheelchairs out on the grass margin, outside the gate of some nursing home or small hospital. There were so many devoted carers. The sick and their carers would be one of the abiding memories.

We were fortunate in being given a choice for the time of year. We couldn't have taken a nicer time than the dawning of a new spring. Seeing the countryside as we started on Easter Sunday morning, the bushes on the roadside still wearing their winter apparel, and finding over a few weeks the whole nation bursting into young life: the greenery, young trees, young plants, the flowers coming along — nature at its very best, between mid-May and mid-June. It was a particularly wonderful experience coming over the 'V' on our way to the Carmelites in Tallow — to see the carpet of purple rhododendrons stretching for miles and miles, right from the top of the 'V' down to the Glen of Aherlow.

There was a tremendous sense of God's power and God's love in the predictably large numbers that continued to come out to every venue, even the smallest and most obscure Carmels. I have a great memory of hearing the Carillon Bells on the side of the cliff overlooking Cobh, sounding out in welcome to Thérèse. But no place stood out more than others. Each place was giving of its very best on the day. There were some places that were outstanding, but there was no place where you felt the visit had been a flop or a failure. Regardless of what preparatory work had been done, it was people power.

DM: You had the privilege of sitting closest to the reliquary for long periods as you travelled through Ireland. What sense did you have as you sat there?

FR RYAN: At times I had to pinch myself, literally, and say, 'This can't be true — not a normal bloke like you — that you should be at the very nub of what the *Sunday Business Post* described as "the greatest mass movement of Irish people in the history of the country".' I kept thinking that God and St Thérèse use the most extraordinary instruments to carry out their goals. It was very humbling. I thought many times of the psalmist who said, 'Unless the Lord build a house, they labour in vain who build it'; and I felt that, whatever labours we had put into the project, it was only the hand of God and the hand of St Thérèse that gave it the magnificence that it ultimately had. If there were bumps on the road, and long hours during the eighty-six days (including travel to and from Lisieux), they were, nonetheless, the greatest days of my life.

There was a lot of administrative work to be done. The Thérèsemobile was magnificently laid out. Two-thirds of it was given over to Thérèse, and then the other section was for the drivers, Pat Sweeney, Jim Doyle and Liam O'Keeffe; in between, I had a little office compartment. We had three mobile phones that were going night and day.

My seat was facing sideways, so at all times I had a view of the reliquary. I prayed a lot. I prayed for the people of each venue. I prayed for my companions, my family and myself. I prayed especially for peace in Ireland, particularly as we travelled through the Six Counties. During the nine-day visit of Thérèse to the North, we were particularly anxious to place the realisation of the implementation of the peace process under her special intercession. We felt that St Thérèse would deliver, and she has. The London *Times* thought it quite extraordinary that we spent nine days travelling throughout the entire North without even the smallest hint of an adverse incident.

It was an extraordinary privilege to spend a number of hours each day in the intimate company of the remains of this beloved saint. I kept saying to myself, 'Utilise this time well; these are moments that will never return. These are moments never to be forgotten — these are precious moments for prayer.' While the phone did distract us, in the quieter moments we all were very conscious of the passenger we were carrying. There were many quiet moments between all of us when we didn't speak for half an hour, because I knew that the others as well as myself were in silent prayer.

You considered the spiritual hunger along the roadside and considered the privilege people felt just to be able to touch the Thérèsemobile, because to them it was a mobile shrine of Thérèse. A woman in Belfast said to us, 'Isn't that her wee house?' We were very conscious that the Thérèsemobile was her home in Ireland when she wasn't in church.

We were sometimes forced to stop, and were delighted to stop in so many places. I know that it worried some people when we arrived an hour, or sometimes an hour and a half, late. Hoping to be at a new venue at two o'clock wasn't always realistic. We very seldom got away from the previous venue on time. While we were very sorry that people would be waiting, there was no way you could pass a hundred or two hundred people on the roadside, sick people in wheelchairs, sick people in cars, who just wanted to touch the Thérèsemobile where the sacred relics of St Thérèse reposed. You were so conscious of the hunger of people for something like that, and you felt, here you were, travelling all of eighty days — what a wonderful privilege! We knew we were on a high, and we savoured it — that's the best way I can put it. We savoured every moment, every bump, every little inconvenience that might have arisen.

DM: You had a mass movement of people at a time when Ireland was faced with the threat of foot-and-mouth disease. Some scientists were publicly calling for no gathering of people through-out the country. How did it affect your plans?

FR RYAN: We were very worried initially, and we took a lot of expert advice, veterinary and otherwise, before we actually finalised the decision to bring the reliquary from Lisieux into Ireland. We were fully prepared that, should there be a problem in any particular region, the local bishop would deal with the pastoral situation and would cancel the visit if necessary. We had no particular worry that we would have to close down the whole visit, but we were prepared for that. I have the utmost respect for Minister Walsh, the Department of Agriculture and so many people who did so much good work to ensure, humanly speaking, that the disease would not spread.

We placed the foot-and-mouth problem in the care of St Thérèse, and from the moment we arrived to the moment we departed there wasn't the slightest touch or hint of a foot-and-mouth problem with the pilgrimage. In fact, one of our great joys was to have been invited by the priests and people of the Cooley Peninsula to come and have St Thérèse celebrate with them, shortly after the lifting of restrictions. They felt very down about the whole thing. They had lost, not only financially, but a whole way of life, and that was a very important moment for us to have arrived at the Cooley Peninsula. We had an absolutely marvellous celebration there. I want to put it on record that, as far as I am concerned, St Thérèse kept foot-and-mouth disease out of Ireland because we placed it under her special care.

DM: Tell me the story about the greyhound.

FR RYAN: Stan Cosgrove, that doyen of Irish vets and a very good friend of mine from Kildare, has a son-in-law connected with the administration of Shelbourne Park. At a meeting, shortly after the relics had been in Dublin, the son-in-law spotted a greyhound that was about to race with a rather run-down muzzle. He was afraid it mightn't be up to standard, so he advised the man who owned the dog to exchange the old muzzle with one of the spare ones that are lying around in case of an emergency. The owner, John, sharply responded, 'By jeepers, I won't. That muzzle touched the relics of St Thérèse!' And the funny thing is, the dog went on to win the race.

DM: What do you hope will be the abiding legacy of the visit of St Thérèse's relics to Ireland?

FR RYAN: I am no prophet. I think those who are in charge of pastoral care would do well to prayerfully discern what lessons are to be learned. The hand of God and the hand of St Thérèse have touched our Irish Church in a very deep way, and we must pause, reflect and try to see what that means. We need, I think, to follow the example of St Thérèse. I feel that we have got to advance in the life of the Gospel, along the lines of St Thérèse. I think the finger of God is pointing to the life of St Thérèse and saying, 'You will honour Me, you will love Me, you will fulfil My heart's desire and save your souls, if you continue to study and implement in your own lives the love and the trust and the prayer and the sacrifice and the way of life St Thérèse is showing you.'

Cardinal Daly, who is a great devotee of St Thérèse, wrote to me after the relics had been left back to Lisieux. I think he put it so well when he said, 'The gatherings of people were marked by reverence, quietness, recollectedness and prayer. The abundance and the quality of Confessions throughout the entire visit also indicate that it was a moment of conversion and a renewal of faith for many.' I can only say I am extremely grateful to God that He blessed our humble efforts.

DM: Can you put the Irish visit in perspective *vis-à-vis* other countries?

FR RYAN: They were very interested in Lisieux about what happened in Ireland. The Auxiliary Bishop, Guy Gaucher OCD, and Père Raymond Zambelli, director of the Lisieux shrine and rector of the Basilica, interviewed me for an hour and a half because they knew that something exceptional had happened. They interviewed me on every aspect of the visit and what I thought had brought out the great numbers. They readily conceded that the three million who venerated the relics — some seventy-five per cent of the total Catholic population of Ireland — was the highest individual figure of any country to date, including France. Obviously, we are a small country, so we talked in terms of the percentage of the total population. Naturally, they were very pleased, but hoped — despite, as I say, the Lord taking it over — they could learn from some aspects of our organisation.

I told him I thought that the choice of the diocesan structure, using the cathedrals as venues around which the whole diocesan parochial system could gather, was a contributory factor to the success. I also said that the Irish people were quite natural night-owls, in total contrast to the people of France, who go to bed shortly after seven o'clock in the rural areas. I said people who came back from work had time to shower and dress up and have their evening meal, and hadn't the constraint of trying to beat a church closing deadline; they knew that, no matter what time they arrived in the evening or into the small hours of the morning, they would find the church open.

We had a solemn re-entry of the relics through the main door of the Lisieux Basilica, and the magnificent bells — very similar to Cobh — rang out in joyful greeting at the return of Thérèse to her home.

'*God gave me a heart which is so faithful that once it has loved purely, it loves always.*'
Thérèse of Lisieux

1

A Shower of Roses

BREDA O'NEILL, TYRONE

My faith in St Thérèse began in September 1996, when my dear husband Aidan died from cancer. He was only fifty years of age. Shortly after his death we had a statue of St Thérèse put in the local church in his memory, as a member of his family happened to have a statue in her home, so we chose to use it. We felt very privileged to have it there, and we prayed to her whenever we visited the church. Little did we know at that time the role she would play in our lives to come.

On 10 July 1999, my lovely daughter Siobhan was involved in a motorbike accident in Inver, Co. Donegal, in which she lost her life. She passed away at the scene of the accident. She was only twenty-three years old and lived life to the full. My family and I were told the terrible news; it was heartbreaking to think I had lost such a wonderful daughter and sister to my other five children.

We had to travel to Donegal that evening to identify her body. Before we got to the hospital where her body lay, we met her friends Sarah and Johanne, who were with her when the accident happened. Sarah handed me a novena leaflet and said, 'Here is a prayer; someone put it in Siobhan's hand at the scene of the accident.' I clung on to it; it was the last thing she held in her hand, and now I had it.

We then left and, with great difficulty, went to see Siobhan. Later that evening my sisters-in-law Ann and Patricia, who were with me at the mortuary, sat with me in the hospital studying the novena leaflet; it had a picture of St Thérèse on the front, and on the back was the picture of an angel dropping rose petals to St Thérèse down below. It was the first time I was told that St Thérèse said she would send down a shower of roses from Heaven. I was then comforted in thinking that she was letting me know that Siobhan's soul was gone to Heaven. This leaflet was her way of telling me.

As the next few days progressed, we had Siobhan's remains taken home. Through the time of the wake I clung on to the novena leaflet because it gave me great comfort. My other five children and I were finally told by the undertaker to say our last goodbyes to Siobhan. Her friend from college, Maria, went and put a medal in the coffin; then my family and I went and said farewell. We walked out the bedroom door heartbroken; but, to my amazement, outside the bedroom door on the carpet lay a lot of rose petals. Again I was comforted; I thought, 'This is St Thérèse helping me along.'

We then went outside the house, the coffin was put in the hearse and all the wreaths were placed on top of the hearse. My family and I and all the mourners proceeded to walk behind the hearse to the chapel, which was about two hundred yards away. As we walked, we were amazed when the rose petals from the wreaths started to blow onto the ground in front of us. I picked some up and held on to them, because I felt St Thérèse was most certainly present.

We had a very sad but beautiful ceremony, and Siobhan was laid to rest where her father Aidan lay. That evening we went to a local club, where we brought our friends for tea and something to eat. While we sat there, my sisters-in-law Ann and Margaret went to my house to check if all was well. When they returned to the club they were all excited. They had a library book which they said they found at the entrance to our home; the title of the book was *Princess Home at Last*, and on the front cover was the picture of a young girl wearing a dress covered in roses. Then Maria realised that the medal she had put in the coffin was one of St Thérèse; she had picked a medal at random from a bunch of medals, and it happened to be that of St Thérèse. Also, I was later to hear from my other daughter, Louise, that Siobhan had got a tattoo of a rose on her back.

In the week following the funeral, post started to arrive and people rang. The first letter that amazed me was from a woman in Donegal, Mrs Campbell, a stranger to me. She told me she learned of Siobhan's accident while in Manchester at her niece's graduation. She happened to be in the house when I rang my other daughter Louise to tell her the terrible news of Siobhan's death — Louise and her niece happened to be friends. She then went on to write that she returned to Donegal, went into a shop in Ardragh and met the woman who had put the novena in Siobhan's hand. So I have since met the woman from Ardragh, and I am extremely grateful to her for what she did and the comfort it brought me and my family.

Many other people I have not named were extremely good and did all they could at the scene of the accident. I would like to say at this point that I ask St Thérèse to send down a shower of roses to each and every one of them. I know they all deserve her help.

On Siobhan's first anniversary last year, I noticed some roses growing through a bush outside my house — they probably came through from the house next door. But this year they bloomed again just before her anniversary. The night before, I was sitting at my living-room window, looking at the roses. I was thinking of Siobhan when suddenly I realised I was looking at Siobhan's picture — it was on the wall behind me, but because of the window it was reflected right into the centre of the roses. I thought, 'Here is St Thérèse again, telling me that Siobhan is safe in Heaven.'

I had the privilege of visiting St Thérèse's relics in Armagh, and I learned later when they were in Donegal they passed the spot where Siobhan's accident happened.

❧

GEMMA JORDAN, CO. DUBLIN

My friend's mother is dying and I went to visit her in hospital. I brought a bouquet of flowers with four roses in there and she told me, with great delight, how she had asked the little Thérèse to bring her roses through a friend.

❧

TERESA BUCKLEY, DOWN

My patron saint is St Thérèse, so I have been interested in her life and read *Story of a Soul*. I live in Newry, Co. Down, and was privileged to see her relics come to the cathedral on 23 May 2001. I must say that at first I did not like the idea of any saint's bones being carted around — I am of the opinion that all should be left to rest — but now I definitely have changed that notion. I now see clearly that St Thérèse's prophecy of 'doing good on Earth and after death letting fall a shower of roses' was being fulfilled.

I had put down my name to help with stewarding, but there were so many helpers that I was not needed, so I waited in the cathedral to venerate the relics. There was a delay as the Thérèse-mobile visited the Cooley Peninsula to help the people come to terms with the foot-and-mouth disease, so I went outside and bought a white rose. I am surprised to see that the rose has now started to grow, so that will be a reminder of the great day.

When the casket was carried up the aisle I felt as if someone was 'hugging my heart', and I realised that the 'Little Way', so simple yet profound, was appreciated by so many. The relics were brought out to the Carmelite convent at ten o'clock, so I went to say goodbye. I was standing with tears in my eyes at the barriers and I said to the lady beside me, 'I am crying with joy because I am called Thérèse.' She said, 'I am named after her sister Céline.' Was it coincidental or a wee message?

Five years ago I had an operation for cancer, and would you believe, it was on the saint's old feast day, 3 October. I am now doing well, so the Little Flower did show her power in that hour.

We have only this life in which to live by faith. We have a saint for most walks of life, but I think St Thérèse is for all.

❧

ANONYMOUS, MEATH

I visited the Pro-Cathedral in Dublin and bought a rose from the street-sellers outside. I touched the casket with the rose and placed it in my shopping-bag, and waited for the Mass and the blessing. On the way home to Ashbourne by bus, I placed the shopping-bag on the floor of the bus.

I have lost my sense of smell for about ten years — I am now an OAP. I started to get waves of perfume around me and I checked the people near me, but it did not appear to come from them — mainly men, and very few people on the bus. Then I thought of the rose, but could not smell the rose. The perfume continued for a short time, but not after I left the bus. I still have the rose, but it is now withered and I have not got my sense of smell back. My petition that day to the Little Flower was not for a personal favour, but for a general favour for Ireland — that may still happen!

❦

GERALDINE SINNOTT, WEXFORD

My personal experience of St Thérèse was a simple one. I followed her reliquary from the church to Bride Street, which was very joyful. The following Wednesday night, at 10 p.m. or 10.30 p.m., I walked down School Street towards Bride Street Chapel. I felt a great sense of wonder. It reminded me a bit of being in Lourdes. It had a great sense of expectation. Yes, I thought, this was something special.

I went in and touched the reliquary and walked home. I was passing the priest's house on School Street when I got a beautiful smell. It was a strong aroma of flowers — it was really beautiful. I came back later on to get that smell again.

I visited the reliquary again when it came to Clonard. After St Thérèse had left to go back home, I picked a rose from her grotto that was in Clonard Church. I brought it home and put it in a vase. I change the water on it every day. Today, 21 August, it's still as fresh as the day I got it. To me that is just amazing.

❦

NOREEN FITZGERALD, LIMERICK

Like many thousands of Limerick people, my daughter and I went to St John's to pay our respects to St Thérèse. The roads were closed to traffic and, despite the rain, people were walking in great numbers as if on a pilgrimage. There was joy, friendship and chat. I thought of when Pope John Paul came to Limerick and we walked through the night to see him. There was the same sense of unity and purpose as we walked to St John's and joined the queue.

While in the queue, a young Dublin lad was walking up and down selling roses. As he was selling the roses, he gave us the following information on St Thérèse:

'Thérèse is going to jail tomorrow, from there she is off to Killarney, and then she is going to Cork and Waterford. From Waterford she is going to England, and from England she is going to Boston in America. From there she is going back up to Heaven.'

An old man in the queue laughed until the tears ran down his face. I'll always associate this young lad's 'masterclass' with my visit to St Thérèse.

❦

DERMOT KELLY, ARMAGH

This is the testimony of two friends of mine, Jim and Sheila Campbell of Arthur's Villas, Armagh. Sheila became interested in St Thérèse about fifteen years ago when a work colleague, whose child had been diagnosed as suffering from leukaemia, gave her a copy of a novena prayer to the saint and asked her to pray for her son.

At that time Jim's sister-in-law, Anna, was found to have breast cancer, and Sheila used the prayer. They were in Dublin with friends the day prior to Anna's operation and, participating in a small group photo at a hotel for the occasion, Jim was handed a rose in the frivolity. He took it as a sign of hope.

They returned home and drove to Craigavon hospital to visit Anna. She assured them she would be all right and was in such good form that both she and Sheila danced along the hospital corridor. Anna had the mastectomy and, despite experiencing much family grief subsequently, she has enjoyed good personal health.

About twelve years ago, Jim experienced a worrying family concern and began a novena daily to St Thérèse. Lacking any sign of a resolution, he asked her for some symbol of hope in the matter. He ended his prayers and proceeded to meet his wife at her workplace. To brighten him up, she handed him a rose given her by a customer earlier. He saw its significance. Within hours the problem was solved and worry lifted. He has lit a candle daily ever since.

Obviously, both are dedicated followers of the saint and were deeply impressed by the visit of her relics — or, as Sheila insists, the visit of St Thérèse — to Ireland. They both participated in the guard of honour at St Patrick's Cathedral and were deeply impressed by the vast numbers and social mix of young people attending the church for the occasion.

As a result of their work they received two tickets to attend the Wexford farewell. They took with them the bib of a baby son of a nephew. This child, the first born after eighteen years of marriage, was in hospital at that time with a serious heart condition, awaiting an operation. Sheila touched the bib to the casket and brought it back for the baby to wear. The child's mother had been doing the novena on Jim's and Sheila's advice. They, in turn, found a rose dropped by chance on the hospital floor during her anxious vigil. Though still today in receipt of treatment, the baby recovered sufficiently to be taken out of intensive care shortly after that incident.

JOHN SHERRY, MONAGHAN

The relic of St Thérèse visited Monaghan on Saturday, 26 May 2001. I bought a small bouquet of flowers at the local shop to place outside on the windowsill, as the relic was to pass by the house *en route* to the cathedral.

Following the visit, the flowers remained fresh for about twelve weeks or more, even though the water had never been changed. They also retained a lovely scent, which remained up until a very short time ago even though the flowers themselves withered.

Just in the last week I had a very severe earache which came on suddenly. I placed the flowers (which are now well withered) to my ear and prayed that the pain would go; it did, and has not returned since.

JOE HEFFERNAN, CORK

When I heard of her impending visit to Ireland, I was a little worried, because during the years I seldom met anybody who had a devotion to St Thérèse. I said to myself, 'Who knows her in this land of the Celtic Tiger?'

The saint has, since her visit to Ireland, become a household name. A new generation of devotees has emerged because of her visit.

Thérèse Martin is my constant companion, my best friend. When her mortal remains arrived at Rosslare to commence her special visit to my country, it was as if my best friend had come to visit me. I told myself that Thérèse was not visiting Ireland for me, but for others. She had visited me many years ago. I felt that Thérèse could give me no more. How wrong I was!

I had journeyed many times to see Thérèse in Lisieux; the saint was now visiting me. I felt humbled but proud also. The Lord tells us that, if we are to boast, then boast about the Lord. Thérèse certainly knew how to boast about the Lord.

The day of her arrival at Rosslare was marked in a special way for me.

I had given up cigarettes for Lent. During Holy Week I found my fast very difficult. On Good Friday, I was craving for one, but I decided to wait until Easter Sunday before having one. I left Cork to journey to Rosslare and arrived fairly early, to discover that the remains would be a little late arriving. I went to the local garage and bought some cigarettes, and they were like magnets drawing me towards them. But I said in my heart that out of respect for Thérèse I would wait until the saint arrived. I have not smoked since. I didn't ask Thérèse to get me off them, but that's how she works.

I did visit the holy remains regularly several times during the saint's special visit to Ireland. On one occasion I brought a friend with me. As I was a little early calling for her, I waited for her in her garden and asked permission to pick some rose petals. I filled a bag of them and brought them to the SMA near Blackrock, Cork. As I walked around St Thérèse, I quietly placed the petals over the casket. At that moment I felt I was offering her the pages of my life and she was accepting them. I knew then also that she had shared every moment of my life with me.

I was moved later to attend Confession, something I rarely do. During Confession my suffering, which had remained hidden from me, was revealed. Thérèse allowed me to see that my suffering had remained hidden from the world and would continue that way. Mankind can be too proud to admit their personal suffering, even to themselves. God allowed me during Confession to admit mine.

I have never asked the saint to send me roses, but during her visit I did request her to send me a rose. I asked her if my love for her was just imaginary or was it genuine; if it was genuine, then she was to send me a rose that very day. The rose did arrive, bunches of them, and continued to fall in the door for several days after.

As a matter of fact, I seldom ask anything of Thérèse for myself, but for others; she always seems to answer my prayers. What I do ask for, for myself, is that the love of God will live in my heart, to make a human being of me and make my daily life worthwhile in the sight of God.

Thérèse needed special intervention from Heaven several times during her pilgrimage on Earth, and without this help from Heaven the world's greatest saint would not have matured to greatness. We need this help too. The visit of the mortal remains of St Thérèse to Ireland was a mission of love by Thérèse, to teach us how to love God as she loves Him. For Thérèse the great works were to begin only after her death. She is so filled with grace, overflowing so much with God's love, that a shower of roses keeps falling on the world. These roses will fall until time is no more.

It was never about reward for Thérèse, it was about love, and her heart and soul were filled with it, even during the dark night of the soul. Every second, every experience of our lives, Thérèse has been there. Thérèse has experienced the same. We can unite each moment of our lives with the life of Thérèse.

Thérèse mothers my soul every second of my life. She teaches me day by day, unfolding the wonders of life to me. The saint's life is the wonder of the world, so wonderful one could write about it forever. The world will read about her forever. Great painters, writers, singers, all help us to arrive at excellence. Thérèse helps us towards what is possible, towards the glory of God, which is man fully alive.

We cannot survive without love; if love ceases, the world will return to ashes. Thérèse teaches us how to love.

❦

MAURA HENRY, GALWAY

After giving birth to four heavy children I developed a major problem with a prolapsed bladder and a prolapsed womb. As the years went by my problems got much worse. As I was very busy, working as a nurse and rearing four children on my own, I had very little time for myself. As my feet gave trouble when I was in training — with the long hours, short staff and constantly standing for sometimes up to twelve hours when on night duty — I developed fallen arches. I can walk fairly well, but not stand in one position; standing still puts more pressure on the feet, especially when there is no arch support. The same with the prolapsed bladder and womb: the backache is there all the time, but much worse when standing.

I travelled to Dublin on Friday 11 May and stayed with my daughter Ellen Thérèse in Bray. Her boyfriend, Sean O'Briain, did the driving to Our Lady's Manor in Dalkey. It was a beautiful day on Saturday, 12 May 2001. The relics were due to arrive at 4.00 p.m. but were delayed in Blackrock. A large crowd had gathered, over a mile long at least. We were standing in the one position without moving an inch for almost five hours. I keep dwelling on this: I stood there in the one spot, with no backache, no pain anywhere — especially those awful feet of mine: never a bit of pain. I found myself telling everyone around me, all total strangers to me. How could I stand with my problems for five hours and not have any pain, or even discomfort?

I was so happy that day; I really felt the healing power of St Thérèse. Another unusual thing happened when I returned home. I was telling a friend of mine I was in Dublin. Her reaction was, 'Ah, my goodness, what day was that?' I told her, 'Saturday, 12 May.' 'Isn't that strange?' she said. 'Twice that day I got the smell of roses; once was early in the day, and again in the afternoon.' She associated this with my visit after hearing my story.

❧

DR DEIRDRE KILLELEA, CLARE
(co-founder of the Panda Foundation, which assists children at risk with various disabilities)

I heard about St Thérèse's tour coming to Limerick a few months ago, and reminded a friend of mine, who is a priest, that when the time came I would like to go to see it at St John's Cathedral. But when the day finally came, I was quite weak after my chemo and its side effects and didn't get much farther than a rather feeble wander around the garden.

My next-door neighbour Kay came out and invited me in for a cup of tea. I was rather poor company, really just wanting to get back into my bed with a water bottle on my churning tummy. Before I left, though, she mentioned that she and her husband were going to visit the relic that evening and would be happy to take me with them. For a moment I thought I would try to go, but then I envisioned the long lines of people who would be there, and knew I wouldn't be able for it. So I told her how much I wanted to see St Thérèse but explained I was too ill to go that day, and asked her to say a prayer for me.

The next day she knocked on my door. She brought me a rose petal — which, she told me, had been around St Thérèse's remains — and a small cream-coloured candle, which I keep in my house.

The following week, quite sick and nauseated from the chemotherapy, with my stomach turned inside out, I prayed to God and to St Thérèse before I fell asleep. 'I hope you won't be too disappointed in me,' I told them, 'but I really don't think I have the strength to raise the money and keep the dream of Panda going. I am just absolutely exhausted and can't imagine how this is supposed to happen. Lord, if you want this to happen, you will have to show me how, because I don't have a clue how to make it happen. St Thérèse, maybe you can explain it to Him for me. I gave it my best shot.' With that, I fell asleep.

The next day, around noon, I was awakened by a telephone call from Don Mullan from 20/20 asking if I would be up to doing a show the following week for Panda due to changes in schedules. Perhaps it was St Thérèse's discussion with God....

❦

EILISH WHITE, ANTRIM

One year ago, on 15 February, my youngest and very precious son Raymond, aged thirty-two years, took his own life. I cannot begin to describe to you our anguish and heartbreak over this. I was totally wrecked with guilt that I had not noticed anything unusual in Raymond's behaviour. He was always a very outgoing lad, full of fun and life. None of us could find any answers. He did leave me a letter, which was some comfort, but still the torture in my mind went on.

I had never prayed much to St Thérèse; it was always the Sacred Heart and Our Lady that I took my troubles to. However, when the relics arrived in Ireland I began to pray to her, and so I was in Clonard monastery the day that her relics arrived. When I went up to the casket I just asked her could she let me know in some way if Raymond was at peace. I thought perhaps I might have got this through a dream.

However, a few days later I was walking down the Glen Road and there on the footpath was a most beautiful basket of red roses. Just a short distance in front of me were walking three women; I don't know how they didn't see this. A whole sense of peace descended on me. I will never forget it, and it has continued with me ever since. I just know that Raymond is at peace now and that he is happy.

The priest in the monastery told us that day that St Thérèse had suicidal tendencies and had great sympathy for anyone who felt that way. I had often heard that if you ever prayed to her and received a rose or a flower, your prayers were being answered. I cannot believe that I have found this peace of mind. I have the basket of roses here in my home.

'I understood that love comprised all vocations, that love was everything, that it embraced all times and places ... in a word, that it was eternal!'
Thérèse of Lisieux

2

A Great Feeling of Peace

ALINA MILLARD, CORK

I went to Sunday Mass to the African Missions Church, Blackrock Road, Cork, in the month of June. I knew the dates the relics of St Thérèse of Lisieux would be visiting the church. I intended to go on the Saturday and didn't make it, so I was extremely glad that Sunday morning to find that the relics were still in the church. At that particular time I had questions about my faith.

In the church, just before the Communion, I said in my mind, 'I believe and know that you are God, but in Heaven only; I don't think you are on this Earth.' I would like to say here that I had a difficult life, even though I am only forty-eight years of age.

Then I felt this tremendous feeling of love. It was indescribable. I can find no words fit enough to describe this feeling I experienced. I can only try to express the great love that I felt. It was over-powering, overwhelming, indescribable love, that I had not experienced before then, and I have not experienced since. I felt like crying after it happened. I came out of the church knowing my question or prayer had been answered, and my faith restored and much stronger than it ever had been in my life.

I would like to thank St Thérèse of Lisieux for this very personal experience. Now I know God is amongst us, and before that I found it hard to believe that he was.

I have never felt anything like this ever in my life.

❧

CATHERINE GERETY, DUBLIN

I was invited to St Thérèse's relics in Kilmacud, Stillorgan. I had to work that weekend and I did not know if it would work out, as I work in a nursing home at weekends, but I put my trust in the Lord and went into work that Saturday, 21 April. The relics were coming at two o'clock and I was finished at two o'clock. I came from work and quickly changed and made up my face, and got a lift to the Carmelites in Kilmacud.

As we were driving up Kilmacud Road we saw a crowd of people standing and people in wheelchairs, walking-sticks, frames, etc. — children, elderly and in between. I got out of the car, said 'bye' and 'thank you' and joined the crowd. I did not know anyone. A lady came up to me and started asking me about myself, and I asked her about herself and we got to know each other. Then I was introduced to others too. I was very happy I came that day.

Then the crowd started to move closer to the convent, and in no time we were in where St Thérèse's relics were. As I got near to St Thérèse's relics, I felt happy inside, but at the same time full of fear and sadness and tightness in my chest. This was because I thought Thérèse would have been laid out; my mother died quite recently, and I find when I go to something like this it brings back all the memories of her illness and being laid out and the deep emotions that lie within my heart. But as I came near my fear and tightness left me. Love and joy and a warm peace came floating into my heart and whole body. I was very happy and cheerful, full of goodness and kindness. Compassion filled my heart, and for many days afterwards it was like she said, 'Go now and share my love and compassion with others.'

I feel I have learned a lot from that special day when I met Thérèse. She is a special friend to me, as I am a small person myself. She believed in small things, and I do small things in my life as I can't do big things — like home help and helping the elderly in a nursing home.

The message I get from her is to be happy and cheerful and contented in life, as life is short. She teaches me to love myself before I can love others. Worry is a useless emotion; worry is like seaweed that pulls you away from trust. I try to trust in God, and when I do trust things work out.

When we got into the Carmelite convent we were welcomed by the Carmelite Sisters with love, joy and peace and understanding too, and no matter if they were tired. The love and faith echoed around the convent hall and outside too.

I met a woman who had worries and problems too. Her name was Geraldine from Stillorgan and she asked me to introduce her to the Sisters and I said I would, so I did. She went home happy, and many others too.

After St Thérèse I went to St Raphael's Convent to say hello to them and call on the Lord too in their lovely chapel. I knelt, I closed my eyes and said my prayer and heard the Lord in my heart: 'Look after my good people,' he said.

Next day I went back to work in the nursing home. I had not even started my work when the nurse in charge said, 'Oh,

Catherine, what a lovely smell!' I asked her what did it smell like? She said, 'Roses.' The shower of roses which Thérèse promised hit our nursing home that day!

❧

Thomas Comiskey, Dublin

Christmas last year, I got very sick with my liver. They told me in the hospital I was dying, and at the time I was. I've been taking heroin for the last twenty years — I'm thirty-five now. I caught HIV from using dirty needles. I was going out with a girl for eighteen years. I spent half that time in prison. While in prison I got sick and was brought to hospital, where all my visitors had to be suited before they came in to me, as I had shingles and they didn't want me to catch anything. But I got afraid and said, 'I don't want this.' The girl I was going with came up to me and said she had enough. Well, to tell you the truth, so had I, and that time I started to look deeper inside for a change. Anyway, she left me and I didn't see her till I got out; and when I did we fought, and I was on so many tablets for the virus and drinking all the time. I'm out two and a half years and have touched no illegal drugs, only the ones that the hospital put me on last Christmas. I blew up so big that they took me in 'cause my liver was failing; the doctors told me that I would have a short time left. That frightened me.

Now, at the time the relics of St Thérèse of Lisieux were going around, and I said I'd like to go to see them. They released me from hospital to go home to die, so I had the hospice nurse coming out to see me every week. I was afraid. The relics were in Whitefriar Street Church and I was asked to go over with a friend of mine, so I did; but something happened when I got to the casket. I felt that I was there on my own, yet there were thousands and thousands there — but I couldn't feel them, just me and the casket. It was a good feeling.

Now, I was attending St Vincent's Hospital liver unit at the time, and I was bad. I was in bed for five months at home, back and forward to hospital. I was working in a FÁS CE scheme and was asked to go to Medjugorje, so I said, 'Yes, why not?' When I went over there I climbed mountains and prayed for direction, and something happened to me. I got some sort of inner peace over there. There's a grave on top of the mountain; I got to it, my name was called twice. I looked around, but there was no one there. The lady I was with heard it, and Paddy too. So it wasn't just me.

I've done some strange things since I came back — not bad things. I looked for direction and I got it. Now I've to learn to live with what I got. I feel I know what happened to me. I wanted change but didn't know how to get it. When I went to see St Thérèse's relics, I felt peace for the first time. I didn't expect what I got. It was strange at first, 'cause I never had religion before. Now it's different: I go to Mass on Sundays and I pray at night, where I didn't do much before.

I got released from hospice care since I came back, Vincent's Hospital released me, and Dr Sheen said I won't have to go back on the drugs for the HIV unless I need to.

❦

VERA AMBROSE, CORK

On Sunday, 24 June 2001 I went to St Joseph's SMA Church, Blackrock Road, Cork. It was about 9.00 in the morning. I went into the church and I stood beside St Thérèse's relics. I asked St Thérèse to heal my anger and pain; I also asked her to help me to say the Rosary and to help me to make certain correct decisions in my life.

As I asked St Thérèse to heal my anger and pain, a great feeling of peace engulfed my whole being and my heart started to flutter. It was as though she was saying to me, 'I am here for you.' I was very moved by this experience and I felt privileged, as I was so happy. I am now saying my Rosary better, or more often, and I know she is there to help me if I just ask her.

I went to see St Thérèse's life story, called *A Shower of Roses*, here in the cinema in Cork on 30 July 2001; the proceeds were for children in Galatha in India. I felt that night St Thérèse blessed each and every one there. Today I feel spiritually very close to her.

❧

MONICA O'SHEA, LIMERICK

I am a forty-eight-year-old woman, married with six children, ages twenty-four years to nine years old. I really didn't know very much about the life of St Thérèse until I had decided, told my family, I was definitely going to Limerick to visit the reliquary. I felt such a strong compulsion to go, especially as I buried my darling mother in late April — she died of cancer, and I missed her terribly.

By coincidence, on the night she passed away, a lovely close family friend brought me the book *Story of a Soul*. I really could not leave the book out of my hand until I had it all read. It was absolutely fantastic — I completely fell in love with this young woman's view of life, her love of God and her complete belief in the Heaven above. I was extremely excited as her visit drew near; I almost felt like a lovestruck teenager going to a pop concert.

My daughter, aged fifteen, came with me and a good friend of mine.

I will never forget the atmosphere outside St John's Cathedral (I went on 18 June 2001, during the evening Mass and Confessions session). We bought the roses to be blessed, and the people in the queues were singing lovely hymns. If you witnessed all the people that received the Blessed Sacrament — it was astounding. Loads of teenagers there and young families. As we filed our way up the church to kiss and touch the reliquary, I really cannot explain the beautiful feeling I had. I kept thinking of her lovely writings; I felt so honoured to be in the same building as her remains.

I was lucky to receive one of the roses that was placed on the reliquary when it entered the Cathedral. I have it wrapped in special paper and I have it placed beside me in the kitchen, where I touch it and the cover of her book when I talk to her. I really do pray and talk to her so many times during the day, silently (otherwise the family would think I was cracking up). If I am upset or worried about something, I immediately talk to her and ask her for help. I always feel so much better and refreshed before the day is out.

She has taught me that saints are just ordinary people doing their work extraordinarily well — no matter if it's only sweeping the floor, doing it as good as you can and doing it cheerfully. I am a sacristan in my local little country church, and I feel like God's little housekeeper and I feel privileged doing it. I've put up an altar to St Thérèse of Lisieux and put up prayers of petition that people might say when they come in during the day to the church. There is nothing as soothing or gives as much pleasure as being alone in the church, cleaning or dusting, and talking to God, our Lady and St Thérèse. Sometimes I almost feel them smiling at me as I'm hurrying around in a terrible rush, trying to get everything done because I'm rushing back to my family to get the dinner etc.

You have only to look at the flowers that grow, the rain, the sunshine, the clouds in the sky, to see God all around you. I feel so refreshed and full of enthusiasm for life since my visit to the reliquary. Bringing the reliquary to Ireland was the best thing I've experienced in my lifetime. Look at the good it done all around the country.

I really do love her — and I tell her so every day, quietly. She was so 'human' about things, wasn't she?

❦

ANN McGAHEY, LOUTH

Five years ago I was diagnosed with breast cancer. I received the appropriate treatment and was doing quite well until February 2000, when I got a pain in my chest. I was referred to hospital for tests. After numerous tests I had my gall bladder removed in December 2000, hopefully to eliminate the problem. Unfortunately, this was not the case; the doctors still could not find out the cause of the pain. At times I thought it was all in my imagination and I was going mad in the head. I am a married lady with five young sons, and both my husband and I had to carry on our normal everyday life with this worry.

I sat up in the Medical Missionaries of Mary late at night. The calm, the peace — I do not even now know how to describe it. I do know I begged St Thérèse to help me: if there was nothing wrong with my health, then let me get on with my life, but if there was a health problem please let the doctors find it. I also visited St Thérèse in Stamullen with the same request, and also had the same overwhelming experience of peace and calmness while in the presence of the relic.

My request was answered, and I was diagnosed with cancer of the breastbone — maybe not the answer I was hoping to get, but the problem was solved, I believe through St Thérèse. I am very much aware my family and I have a very tough road ahead, but hopefully with everyone's prayers and St Thérèse's help we will get there.

I cannot explain the feelings I had in the presence of the relic, but I do know it was a once-in-a-lifetime experience and hopefully will carry us through some dark days.

❦

ANONYMOUS, DUBLIN

When I went to see the relics of St Thérèse I did not know what to expect. I was curious about it and was wondering what it was all about. I went to a few different venues. At first, when I was there, I looked on and said to myself it was all very new to me. I watched people, young and old, the sick — I was amazed to see so many people, and all showing great respect and reverence. I was delighted to see that people made the effort to come, for whatever reason — it didn't matter: once they came, St Thérèse would do the rest.

The second place I went to see the relics was a different experience for me. I stayed for a few hours. Something much deeper happened for me there, and I am sure it was because I spent much more time there and had space to reflect. At this time I had a lot going on in my life and my heart was just broken with pain. I didn't realise that the heart could hurt so much. When I was with the relics, I knew that St Thérèse went through pain and that she understood. She gave me great comfort. I felt I was taken away to a quiet place and my heart was given a rest from pain. When you are hurt, you can bring God into it, and then you can see clearer the need for God's light. It was like my heart was brought out to the sunshine and the rays of the sun healed the broken heart. It brought peace and happiness. It brought me a peace that this world cannot provide. The pub, disco, etc., could not bring me this peace, because I had tried it. I was touched by the people who were there also, and there was a great sense of peace.

St Thérèse is a sign of hope — she has refreshed me and many others. She knows what it's like to live on this earth and how difficult it can be. She is there as an example to us all and as a friend. Thanks to St Thérèse and to God for the privilege of being part of this great visit of hope.

❦

ANONYMOUS

Long before St Thérèse was to come to Ireland I started going through all my old prayers and Bible books. I started to do her prayers etc., and I was in Prague last Christmas, so I thought when I heard St Thérèse was coming it seemed I was meant to see her. I honestly didn't think half as many would feel the same; how wrong I was!

I was scared to pray to her, because I heard people say if you pray to St Thérèse you always get crosses. I had enough, and my life is upside down — or was. I didn't know what to do. I got so tired praying and not getting answered. Days I went home exhausted, saying, 'God, are you there? I'm not asking for very much....' Days and nights I cried with hurt, anger, loneliness — you name it, I felt it.

I decided to go to Derry when the relics came, but my car was broke and I didn't get there. Then I said I'd go to Letterkenny — didn't get there either; my car was still in the garage, I couldn't afford a taxi, and I wouldn't go on my own anyway. But something told me I had to go to the relics.

I phoned Nora on Sunday to see if she would go to Bruckless with me. So off we went. On the way Nora and I had a great talk, helping each other with our problems. I said to Nora, 'We don't even know the way, but all roads lead to home and home again.' I told her I had to go. 'I have to see the light. I need help.'

We talked and laughed, not expecting anything. When we got there the queues were getting longer and longer. It started to spit a little and it was getting cold, but everyone was delighted the rain stayed away. While we were standing, a lot of people were going in on the right who had medical problems etc. I said to Nora, 'Do you notice there's not a sound from the wains [kids]?' They were all ages from babies up.

When we got our turn to the relics, I was feeling scared to do it wrong (I have no confidence at all) and scared to keep people waiting if I touched it the way I wanted — I wanted to kiss it. I had so many roses in my hand and beads I bought. When we sat down after, Nora said, 'Look what's in the wee prayer we got, about the light to see — what you were talking about coming up.'

Going out the door, I said, 'Nora, I don't know if I touched the relics.' I touched the roses and my beads, but I don't think I touched it with my hand. Nora did the sign of the cross on my forehead and

said, 'There, I touched it.' But the second she did it I felt something.
My head was sore — it was like the way when people say about a
faith healer. And this lovely little drizzle of rain was falling — it was
lovely, lovely — and next minute the sun came out, at eight o'clock,
and we could feel this lovely warm feeling on our necks and faces.
We couldn't believe it. And straight in front of us was this beautiful
big rainbow from one end to the other. That night, going out with
our friends, we started to tell them about it. Nora said, 'Aye, and
we were able to look straight at the sun and it never even hurt
our eyes.'

The sun went in when we got into the car, and going along the
road we kept on about it. It was so strange: the sun came out again,
and I saw this lovely altar made to St Thérèse. So I pulled over and
got out. I'd swear she was smiling at me, and I said, 'You are
beautiful.'

I think Thérèse is trying to help me sort out my life. It's such a
mess. Next day Nora called down to see me. She couldn't believe
the difference in me. I knew exactly what I want to do now, if it
works out for me; at least I got my head out of the sand and started
getting things seen to that I hadn't in the last five years.

I know St Thérèse helped me. I can't say yet how it will go, and
I need to pray more to her than I am. I'm still a little scared; but, as
I said to Nora, your Father can't hand you a snake when you ask for
some wee thing. I was meant to go there, that I know.

Also, this is strange to me. The house I'm in now, I'm here almost
nine years now. The very old rosebushes wouldn't come out in
bloom — they came out more or less withered, and I was lucky if I
got five to ten roses each year. Since the relics, the rosebushes are
all falling over (I must get them tied up) with roses.

❀

ANNIA NÍ SCANLON, SLIGO

St Thérèse's relic arrived in Sligo on Sunday, 3 June. My son Christian and I cycled by the cathedral that sunny afternoon. There was lots of people waiting around. My son Christian asked me what was going on. I told him about her relic. We just moved back from Montana to live here since July 2000. I asked him if he would like to go see her relic. He said maybe.

Monday evening, my older sister Maura was going down at 11.00 p.m. to visit the relic. We got ready to go with her. We fixed some flowers from a wedding bouquet I caught on Saturday night at a relative's wedding — it was a miniature bouquet. And off we went, only to find very long queues, three people abreast, on the street, reaching as far back as the middle of John Street. I asked Maura to return us home, as it would take forever to get in to see her. We returned home; Christian and I talked about getting up at 5.30 a.m. and going down on our bikes. We set the alarm, though not noticing the time had stopped. Got to bed and prayed: *if God wants us there, we will be there.*

Tuesday morning, woke up 5.00 a.m., before the clock should have gone off. Noticed the clock had stopped. I moved with abundant energy that morning; Christian too. We got on our bikes with our bouquet of flowers and our wee list of petitions. It was a beautiful morning, very warm and serene. We got down to the cathedral, parked our bikes inside the church. There was only a handful of people there. Very quiet and peaceful.

When we got to her relic, I placed the bouquet of flowers with the petition note on the handle of the casket. I stood for a moment with my son, and when I touched the casket I felt an overwhelming sense of love and humbleness. I fell to my knees in front of the casket to pray. I asked her to help me walk in Jesus' footprints and to help me love unconditionally.

People were coming all around the casket and tripping over my feet. A lot more people had arrived now. I got up to walk down with my son, when I felt this overwhelming love come over me and I started to cry. My son looked up at me in great concern. I said to him, 'I am crying for joy.' Christian replied, 'Mom, I thought you were sad.' 'No, Christian, joy is feeling the overwhelming love St Thérèse had for Jesus.' We went back to our seats, sat a while and revisited the casket, giving it a kiss before we left.

By noon that day St Thérèse's relic was to leave Sligo, so I was at the front door of where I worked. I saw the most beautiful bouquet of salmon-pink roses scattered against the right inside gate. I went in and picked them up, nine roses in all. I found a vase and placed them in water, and when they had withered I took the tops of the flowers home. Have them on a hankie in my prayer room. They dried beautifully, almost like someone purposely preserved them.

Today I know that overwhelming feeling of love she had in her heart and soul for humankind. Always looking within, reaching for the power within to heal the world — a power in us but not of us. I am blessed to have been in her presence. Her relic left, but her unconditional love remained in my heart.

❦

MARGARET GALLAGHER O'BRIEN, WEXFORD

I always had a special place in my heart for the Little Flower, and when she was coming to Gorey myself and my daughter Noreen, who has Down's Syndrome, left our house at 12.30 to wait for her to arrive in Gorey. Her mobile broke down, so she didn't arrive till 4.00 p.m.; normally I couldn't stand that long, but that day the time standing there meant nothing and the time went by very quickly. The crowds were great — it reminded me of Wexford winning the All-Ireland!

When she arrived, I don't know why but I fell to my knees and I do not remember doing it. The peace I felt was so intense. I felt happy and sad at the same time, so emotional. Then we made our way down town to St Michael's, where we had prayers for her arrival, then prayers for the sick, then the all-night vigil prayers. I went home after the prayers for the sick at 8.30, to get my daughter Noreen to bed for school next day, but for some reason I felt so very guilty at leaving St Thérèse and I could not sleep. So at 5.00 a.m. I got up, got a cup of tea and went to St Michael's to stay with her, and at seven o'clock got Mass. Then I went home to get my daughter to school, and I couldn't wait for to go back to St Michael's. I went up at 11.00 a.m. to get a good seat with my husband John. The Mass was beautiful; then when it was over we followed her to the outside of town to say goodbye. I cried bitter; it was to me like when I was saying goodbye to my own sons, when they were leaving to go back to England.

In 1990 my son Owen, twenty-two years, was killed in England by a bus. My [first] husband got sick and was sick for eighteen months, and died on his fifty-second birthday, 17 October 1992. In April 1993 my father died, and four months later my mother died. So in two and a half years I lost a husband, son, father and mother. I don't know how I managed or where I got the strength from, but I did, and it was with prayer. I pray a lot. I could not live without the Church or prayer.

St Thérèse gave me so much peace in my heart. I am coping so much better now. I went with John and Noreen to say goodbye to her in Rosslare church. It was a beautiful experience for me; I will never forget it for the rest of my life.

❧

KATHLEEN O'CONOR (deaf-blind adult)

I was great privilege with the Deaf-Blind Group Leader Mrs Frances O'Grady to be invited to visit at Thérèse, Flower of Jesus, of Lisieux, by the Carmelite convent, Kilmacud. Was held last April. At first I thought that on special evening was so wonderful and peaceful atmosphere. How I lifted to feel in my heart spiritual of love; and I touched the glass casket to heal my injury, arm and hand, fingers, and now they back to normal again. Thank. And I have the medal of relic of St Thérèse and hang up at my bedside, and begin to devout and prayers to her every day since I visited her. So I appreciate St Thérèse to visit the Irish people and encourage to spread of faith and believe to God and make the great majesty to grow strong faith in Ireland.

❧

FLORENCE MCCABE, LAOIS

My husband and myself were on a visit to Limerick (very un-expected) and heard the novena was on. We went to the penitential service. I had a number of personal worries at that time and I talked to a priest. He remarked, 'You are very troubled; I will pray for you.'

We left shortly after. As we were walking up the street, we noticed cars and traffic, and someone remarked it was the relics of

St Thérèse. As she passed I felt a great sense of peace and calm come over me, and I felt as if all the worries had been lifted off my shoulders.

Some time after, my husband gave me the St Thérèse leaflet, with the prayer that includes the words, 'A Father's love watches over us each day of our lives' — and I feel great trust and confidence in God's words, and the worry has never returned. If at times I do get down, I recall the day in Limerick and again feel at peace and able to trust in God.

❦

GERALDINE MELIA, KILDARE

In March 1997, the family joined Dad for his retirement party (from BWG Foods). He retired early at fifty-nine years of age, to spend extra time with his wife and family. He planned to travel with Peggy (his wife) and visit us all, play golf, catch up with friends and relax. His colleagues hugged their friend and thanked him for the motivating effect of his amazing energy levels, his honesty, kindness, good humour and humanity.

Little did we guess what was ahead of us, as we danced and laughed. Within six months, Dad's life changed dramatically.

At 4.00 a.m. on 27 September 1997, he had a stroke. Two days after the stroke, the doctor said that Dad was paralysed (left-hand side), he was haemorrhaging, some brain tissue was damaged, his vision and speech were affected. Dad would have to lie flat for some time. It was too dangerous to operate. The doctor said that, at best, Dad would be in a wheelchair; that all we could do was sit and wait. Everything seemed unreal.

Dad joked a lot. He spoke to each of us about our lives and our future. Dad said that he was determined to get well and that 'something good will come from this'. He had blind faith in God; he believed that he would live through this — and he did.

We tried our best to create a positive atmosphere in his room. We drew up a rota and stayed with Dad twenty-four hours a day. He held our hands and patted our heads. The doctors said that touch seemed to be important to him and to stay with that contact, so we did. Night in, night out, we slept in the hospital and held his hand.

The haemorrhaging eventually stopped. After three weeks, Dad was allowed to sit up in bed. Physical and speech therapies started at this stage. Three months after the stroke, Dad was allowed to come home for a few days on Christmas Eve 1997. During Christmas dinner he thanked us all for supporting him through this tough time. That day was a real mixture of happiness and sadness. We were all so glad that he could be with us, and yet we were aware that life had changed. I was not the only one at the table who let some tears fall down my face discreetly.

Over the last four years, Dad has spent his time in hospitals, Dun Laoghaire Rehabilitation Centre, nursing homes and at home being cared for by his family, who would do absolutely anything for him — and, as he says himself, he is worth it!

Life has not been easy for Dad, but he rarely complains — he prays. There have been crises along the way, but none that caused Dad to lose faith.

Last year, Dad went through a particularly tough time that started on 23 December 1999. He had another minor stroke and was admitted to hospital. The next eight months passed in a haze of hospitals, our home, nursing homes and one crisis after the next.

Dad had minor strokes, pneumonia three times, experienced pain, infections and had complications due to diabetes. We now knew that food was entering Dad's lungs when Dad ate. Then the doctors told us that they would have to operate, to put a tube in his stomach to feed him — that the gag had not corrected itself, and if Dad ate or drank, food would go to the lung, he would most likely become seriously ill again.

Dad just accepted everything, and we noticed that he had become extremely peaceful. In fact, we often said that his room became a real place of calm and serenity. There was always a positive feeling in the room. He told us that he prayed for us all every day.

We knew he missed the food. He began to admit it as time went on. It was getting difficult for him. He wanted a drink, 'just a sip of water', but it was too dangerous to give it to him. He began to tell us how difficult it was not to eat or drink or go to the dining-room with the others. On warm days in May this year, he was really thirsty and constantly wanted a drink just to quench the thirst.

In 2001, before St Thérèse's relics came to Ireland, Dad developed a major interest in St Thérèse (he had always had her relic and prayed to her). He told us he had a dream — St Thérèse was in it; he told us all to visit her and pray to her. Leaflets and posters about St Thérèse took over the room. He constantly spoke about her and had her tour details on the wall. He listened to all the news about her on TV and constantly checked for the date of her arrival. As time got closer, he insisted that he wanted to be taken to the relics.

We were advised that we could take him, but that he might be weak and want to return straight away. We decided to take the chance — it seemed so important to him. My mother took him with the help of relatives. Dad stayed two hours and prayed. Mammy told us later that he was very peaceful, and that she could not believe that he wanted to stay there so long. He asked to be taken up to the relics twice. When he returned to the hospital, he was very peaceful and prayed a lot. He told everyone to make sure and visit the relics.

When Thérèse's relics left Ireland, someone tried to take the tour details down from my father's wall; he told them to leave it there. He continued to talk about St Thérèse. It was great to see him with an interest again. We all noticed a remarkable increase in energy — like a new lease of life.

On 13 July 2001, I phoned Dad. It was my birthday. He told me that he had great news, that it might be Friday the thirteenth but it was lucky for some: he had been allowed to drink 5ml of water! He was thrilled. I could not believe it. This contradicted all the instructions we had been given for the past year. I told Dad that this was the best birthday present that I could receive. I felt a knot in my stomach — something about the significance of 5ml of water. It was so small, yet such a major milestone in our lives that day. I was nearly afraid to hope that this long and difficult phase for Dad might pass. My mother confirmed that the doctor had checked the gag — it seemed to be perfect.

A few days passed. I phoned Dad again, and he told me that he had had a fruit-of-the-forest yoghurt! He described the taste and told me it was gorgeous. I think I cried and laughed at the same time. He was so excited. The atmosphere on the phone was so light-hearted, and I knew that a weight was lifting off us all. We'd accepted the situation while it was there, but now that there was a chance that it was about to change, I realised the energy and space it had taken in our lives since last July. I asked Dad how he felt and he said that he was thanking St Thérèse — that he knew it was her doing. He had no doubt about this.

The next time I called Dad he had had liquidised food and was joining others in the dining-room. His voice sounded so strong on the phone, like it did before the stroke. He was so happy and told me to say a prayer to St Thérèse.

Dad now gives daily thanks to St Thérèse. The nursing home may decide to stop feeding him through the tube, because he will put on too much weight if he eats both ways! Dad absolutely refuses to allow any details about St Thérèse to be removed from his room; he has absolute blind faith in her ability to heal us, and encourages us all to remember that.

So Dad's positive words in the first week of the stroke have been fulfilled. He admits that his retirement is not as he planned it, but recently I chatted to him and he told me that this is God's way. He said that he wanted to get time with his family and he is getting that, even though it is not in the way he expected. We sit by his bed and we each have plenty of time to chat to him about the things that matter. Maybe, if Dad was not paralysed, we could not all meet in his room; we might be rushing around, without time to talk and without the time to tell each other we care.

We do not plan ahead. We enjoy the present. Dad tells us to pray to St Thérèse for anything we want, that she will listen and answer our prayers. He is living proof of that!

❧

CAITRÍONA FOGARTY, DUBLIN

The whole visit of the relics of St Thérèse moved me greatly, had a profound change in my perspective on life and especially love. I also felt a deep sensation of warmth when I touched the casket, a feeling which I had never experienced before and one which I am sure was a direct experience of St Thérèse's and God's love. I feel extremely privileged to have been touched in this way, and I want to share that with others. I feel that we, the Irish people, are very fortunate to have had an opportunity to share this love, and I hope that through this we can help others.

I had heard of the impending visit of the relics through my mother, and had made no plans to visit. Nothing could have prepared me for what I was about to experience, as I had no expectations or knowledge of the life and love of this wonderful saint.

I queued with others outside the Carmelite convent; there was a wonderful sense of companionship and friendship as people waited expectantly. Once inside the convent church, I touched the casket and felt the most amazing feeling of calm and love. I was offered a rose from the foot of the altar and touched this against the casket to keep as a symbol of what I had just experienced. I knew that up till then I had only been passing through life; I had failed to see the beauty that surrounds me every day. St Thérèse touched me and awakened me to this beauty.

I was drawn back again to the night vigil that evening, and again to the Mass the next day. I was lucky to get a place to kneel at a pew. I was later joined by a wonderful family, a little disabled boy in a wheelchair, his mum and little sister aged about five. The little boy couldn't walk or talk. During the Mass he cried out and moaned lightly, as if he understood exactly what was happening and was crying out in answer to God. Each time he cried, his little sister held his hand, stroking it lightly and soothing him. She rubbed his hair and whispered into his ear, comforting him in his pain. This was the most amazing experience I have ever had of pure love, from sister to brother; it was such a simple expression of love that I shall remember it constantly and be constantly reminded of it wherever I go. Each time the little boy cried out, she was there, reminding me that God is always there for us, whenever and wherever we need him. We only have to ask. This was a revelation to me.

❦

MARY O'SULLIVAN, WICKLOW

Honestly, I wasn't pushed about the visit of the sacred relics at all. Moving statues and all that leave me a bit cold. My interest was stirred by the attention that our Carmelite orders were getting. I have a lot of time for the Carmelites. I was privileged to meet the contemplative Sisters in my local convent in Delgany in a professional capacity some years ago. I was immediately impressed by their spirituality, humanity and, not least of all, their humour — essential ingredients for a decent life, I thought. Now, when I visit, I continue to experience something deep and personal in my prayer there. My interest was further fuelled by the Pilgrimage of Grace. I have felt the grace of God in my own life and witnessed it in others. I have experienced it in a special way since I lost a baby several years ago. I called her Grace. Already the visit was speaking to me.

Word went around the parish of Kilquade that the relics were coming to Delgany. A pilgrimage was arranged from my village of Kilcoole. I was organising my father's surprise seventieth birthday party. Would I even get to Delgany at all? But miracles were already happening.

My dearest aunt confirmed that she would be able to come to the party. I was delighted, especially since illness had kept her housebound for almost a year. Prayers kept her company and in touch with us. Now, she was determined to make the trip by bus from Donegal, crutches and all. Then I realised that she would be here at the same time as the relics. I knew how much it would mean to her to visit them. How would I manage it? Would she be able? I handed it over to God.

Saturday 28 was a typical April day — sunshine and showers. My aunt had arrived safely the previous evening and I was taking her to lunch in Avoca Handweavers. I decided to travel via Delgany, aware that the relics were arriving there that day. I was concerned about my aunt having to manage on the crutches. I need not have worried. No sooner had we turned the corner up the avenue to the convent when a steward directed us along another path. 'Go straight up,' he invited. I felt a bit of a fraud behind my aunt — me, in full health, jumping the patient queue of many familiar faces from my parish. I was relieved for my aunt.

Once inside, everything happened so quickly. Like the great moments of my life, I wanted to pause and stay, to savour and seize each moment. There was stillness and awe and something ethereal in the air. Others felt it too, I have since learned. My aunt was in front of me; I wanted to hold on to her. But this was a personal journey.

My turn: What do I do — say? Feeling awkward. Placing my hands on the reliquary, the prayer came: 'Heal through my hands if it is meant to be.' I was training in reflexology. In my head, a rush of emotion and then peace.

I became aware of my aunt. As she moved away, someone handed her a rose. She was overwhelmed. We sat for a while, shed a tear and prayed in silence.

'I feel so unworthy,' she whispered. When did that happen to us, I thought? When did we learn to be unworthy of love and kindness — to be always giving and then deny it to ourselves? When did we learn to feel bad about ourselves? A legacy from some other age, I am sure. Thank God for the spirit of compassion and mercy which reminds us that we are indeed truly loved as we are. Then I realised that my aunt was moved by the very same thing which moved me on my first visit to Delgany convent — unconditional love.

Then I remembered the roses my mother received on completing her 'special novena'. Those times of her deep prayer, which we respected in our home. Times when she was loving us silently. She must have experienced grace, too, for the struggle with MS, which incapacitated her adult life.

I thought that love has always been there. I have been loved when it must have been hard to love me. Trauma can block out the experience of being lovable and of being able to love. Somewhere I learned guilt and hardness and cynicism and judgement and despair. It had seeped into my bones and my attitude, and no amount of prayer seemed to shift it. But here, on the Pilgrimage of Grace, in the spirit of St Thérèse, beside my lovely aunt, I felt warm and forgiven and loved.

Isn't that what we need? In this age of the individual, to come together as a community for a common purpose in the presence and wisdom of those who have gone before us. In that atmosphere, miracles do happen — call them coincidences, strange happenings, energy, whatever. Can anyone explain how the Sisters provided twenty roses on the day and yet there was an endless supply? Some people came with roses, but never enough to supply so many.

My aunt gave me her rose. I shared its petals with friends. It is difficult to pass a rose without experiencing its warm and nurturing scent. We were awestruck.

Well, we had a great party for my father the following day, and my aunt returned home, still dazzled by our good fortune with the relics.

Why did so many people, of all ages, flock to the relics of St Thérèse? Many felt it would be a great honour and an experience to pass on to their children. In spite of falling church attendance, clearly the need for a spiritual experience did much to bring communities together. It brought many in contact with the Carmelites, who have historically had their finger on the spiritual pulse of the time. In a turbulent society, which is changing too fast for most of us, once you experience that 'something special' there is no turning back. I know now, there is a place I can go for quietness, just to be with myself, as He made me. I needed to be reminded.

🌹

ANGELA MULCAHY, WEXFORD

I lost both my parents about four years ago to cancer; they both had cancer together and both died within three months of each other. I never got over their death. I miss them both so much. I know what pain is, I know what loneliness is. I've been on that roller-coaster with the ups and downs in my life.

When I heard that the relic of St Thérèse was coming to Ireland, I was very excited about it. I drove to Rosslare with a friend to meet her coming onto Irish soil. I took a few days off work to be with the relic. I was lucky: every time I went to see the relic, the seat nearest the relic always became available. I stayed five to six hours with her each time. I am a person who can't keep my eyes open after ten o'clock, and here I was sitting with the relic until 4 a.m. and not wanting to go home. I felt an inner peace and blissfully happy. I just felt possessed by love, going above myself, through excess of fervour and ecstasy. There is no living in love without some pain or sorrow.

The bishops and priests ask, 'What was the message of St Thérèse? What is she trying to tell us?' Well, I believe her message is loud and clear. She is telling us to go back to the simple ways. She is saying if you've got love in your heart you are very close to God, because God is love. God walks with the simple and reveals himself to the humble. Everyone is searching for something; they don't know what's right any more. Millions of people turned out to see the relic, and that touched hearts — so many good people from all walks of life. It gave young priests hope; they know they have to reach out to the people. I never saw the priests so happy. You could feel love all around you, and everyone was happy. You just felt a wonderful, warm, peaceful aura around the place. It's a great feeling.

I spent ten days with her and it was a tonic. This is all I can share with you — nothing exciting, no big miracle, but she left me with peace in my heart. What more could I ask for?

❧

TEENIE McGARRY, ROSCOMMON

My mother's name was Thérèse, and all her life she had a special devotion to 'the Little Flower'. This she passed on to me, along with the name Thérèse. When I was a young girl and heard so much of the goodness of this young saint, I tried (unsuccessfully) to model my life on her life. I even contemplated becoming a nun at one time. These feelings evaporated when I grew up and met 'the man of my dreams', who I married. My spiritual friend and confidante was always the Blessed Virgin Mary, who has always been my lifeline through many trials and tribulations, so I called my first daughter Mary (beautiful name). My second daughter got the name Thérèse as her second name. I have a granddaughter called Thérèse, a divine goddaughter (a woman now) called Thérèse — all these 'Little Flowers' in my life!

When I heard that the bones of St Thérèse were coming to our cathedral in Ballaghadereen, a surge of joy went straight to my heart. At last I would actually be able to see and touch the casket wherein the bones of my patron saint lay.

When the appointed day of arrival (6 June 2001) came, I decided I would go into the cathedral an hour and a half before the due time, to get a front seat. I was not the only one with that idea. When I got there the front seats were gone. I was happy with a seat in the second row. Soon the cathedral began to fill up. There was a low murmur of voices, as people met who had not seen one another for a long time. I myself met some old friends I had not seen for years. Everyone looking happy, in anticipation of the coming of the bones of St Thérèse.

Suddenly there was a hush as the golden casket was wheeled up the aisle silently by some FCA men and followers. It was received so quietly and serenely — no prayers, no ceremony. You could see the awe and adoration on the faces of the people. I myself felt so overcome with emotion, my only release was tears of joy at being there.

After a while the little Holy Communicant children, in their best attire, filed past the casket with reverence, so unusual in children so young. Then the adults followed suit. So many people, in such an orderly procession, touched, kissed, the casket and passed on. Young people, old people, people in wheelchairs, babies in their mothers' arms, sick little ones helped by a parent to touch or kiss the casket.

When my turn came I was transfixed. I placed a little picture of St Thérèse on the casket and felt I was looking into her very eyes with a powerful feeling of love and peace, and I prayed and prayed from my very heart. She had to hear me. It was so emotional. I came away happy.

The cathedral remained open all night. I went back again and stayed until dawn. Twice more I touched the casket. There were roses everywhere, quiet church music in the background, serenity and tranquillity all around. You could feel the goodness and respect of the people, as if they were saying, 'We are all here together on a mission of love and thankfulness to St Thérèse.'

The reception the bones of St Thérèse got everywhere in Ireland — this young girl who lived a short life and died for her love of God — is a message in itself. There is so much goodness and love in the people of Ireland. If it could only be tapped (for want of a better word), maybe it would overcome the hate and bitterness we have in one little corner of our (otherwise) beautiful country. The people are waiting and searching for peace and harmony. Maybe at last St Thérèse will send us the shower of roses she promised.

'… a mother's heart is more discerning than a doctor's, for it knows how to guess at what is suitable for its child's sickness.'
Thérèse of Lisieux

Above: Thérèse, aged eight, with her sister, Céline.

3

Help in Time of Need

JOAN RIGNEY, LOUTH

Before I was cured by St Thérèse, I was so weak and in such pain I could not move. I spent three or four months lying in bed, not able to turn, sit up or get out of bed. The pains in my legs were something else.

On Sunday night before I was cured, at about 10.30 p.m., I saw a vision of St Thérèse standing in the corner of my room beside the wardrobe. My granny was with her. I got a terrible fright and I covered my head with the quilt. After a few minutes I peeped out. The vision of my granny had gone, but I could see St Thérèse there. After a few minutes a cloud came over her and she faded away.

Something kept telling me I had to go out to Our Lady of Lourdes where her relics were. I tried several times but failed. Then on Monday morning, with the help of my husband, I got down the stairs on my bottom. With a lot of struggling and moaning, my husband got me to the car, lifted in my legs. We drove out and we parked outside Lourdes where her casket was. I tried to get out of the car but was unable. My husband seen a Garda and called him to help. He called two other Guards, and with their help I got out of the car and across the road. When I got in to where her casket was,

I got weak, and they helped me to sit down on a chair just across from her casket. They tried to get me up to walk around the casket, but I could not even stand. Then they dragged my chair across to the casket. After a few minutes a nun came with a wheelchair. They tried to get me into it but failed. They then pulled me, sitting in the chair, up to the end of the casket. I sat there for a few minutes.

It was 9.20, and I said to my husband, 'Try and get me out to the car before Mass starts,' as I knew I would not be able to stay for Mass, I was so weak. We came home and he got my son to help me into the house. I sat in the armchair for about one hour. I had a cup of tea and I said, 'See if ye can get me upstairs,' but I could not lift my legs to get upstairs. I then turned around and sat on the second-last step; my son kept my feet pressed on the step so that I would not slip. My husband was behind me, pulling me up each step. After a lot of struggling and moaning I got up to bed.

The following morning I said to my husband, 'I slept all night.' Could not believe it. I asked him to get me a glass of cold water from the fridge. I said, 'Leave it on the locker and I'll try and get it in a minute,' as I could not drink it lying down. He went down to make me a bowl of porridge. I tried to get up to reach the glass of water; but, to my amazement, I just sprang up, drank the water and lay down. Could not believe that I was able to get up, so I tried again and was able to get up like a shot. I then tried to stand up. I stood up straight away and stood looking out the window.

My husband came in with the porridge and I was in tears. I said, 'I'm cured! I can get up, stand and look out the window.' He said, 'See if you can walk.' I stood and walked without any help to the bathroom.

And I'm still flying about the place. I can go down the stairs on my own and up without any help, thank God. I'm still in shock; so is all my family. I have no pains in my legs whatsoever, after years and years. I have no thirst and my diabetes is under control. My blood sugars this morning were 5.2 and they were never out of the twenties — I mean, as high as thirty-three. My weight was twenty stone six pounds the morning I was cured; I'm seventeen stone two pounds today. I feel great. I'll never be able to thank St Thérèse, Padre Pio and St Martin for all their help.

❦

ANONYMOUS, WICKLOW

I was attending a specialist for a cancer mole on my face. I was amazed: after one rub of the blessed rose petal it went completely, after four years. I consider that a cure.

A man in church asked my husband to pray for him, as he had an appointment with his doctor — suspected cancer of the colon. I sent him a petal and prayer to St Thérèse. The doctor asked him, 'What have you been doing?' 'Nothing,' this man said. 'Because,' the doctor said, 'I have a letter written for you to be admitted to hospital, but now I can't see any trace of cancer.' So he told the doctor about the rose petal of St Thérèse. 'Well,' the doctor said, 'these things do happen.'

❦

FRANCIS MCDONAGH (AGE 11), WEXFORD

I had many happy visits to the relics of St Thérèse. My first two visits were to New Ross and I was very excited. I had never been in such big crowds. My mother bought me a lovely statue of St Thérèse and my daddy bought me a lovely framed picture. I used my white cloth to touch the casket on each visit.

I went with my parents in May to South Africa with the Irish Polocrosse Team to visit my brother Aiden, and I brought him one cloth and a picture and a rosary beads. When I came back I was very sick with a touch of malaria. My mother rubbed my face and body with the cloth that touched the relics, and I was much better the next day. St Thérèse cured me.

I have so many different pictures of her and some lovely prayers on the back. I have a little book of the Little Flower and I have read it many times and I have coloured in the pictures at the back. I love the prayer service on page thirty-four. My favourite picture is St Thérèse on her First Communion Day. I am being confirmed on 1 May 2002 and I am taking 'Martin Aiden' as my confirmation names.

For the final service at Wexford my aunt has me on video touching the casket in the GAA grounds. I was very excited to be there, joining in the singing. The balloons were lovely around the grounds. I was very sad when the helicopter took away the casket. We all sang 'Now is the hour for me to say goodbye'. I went to Lady's Island to see the boat in Rosslare that the relics sailed on. Everybody was so happy and said many prayers when the relics were here in Wexford.

❦

JOSEPHINE KEALY, DUBLIN

For several years I have had an awful pain in my back, up near my shoulder-blade. Rest would relieve it a bit, but as soon as I'd bend over the sink or likewise, the pain was back again. Painkillers didn't work. The doctor said it was a muscle in spasm, and I got other pills, but all in vain. Back massage helped a little. It was so bad this year that I had to have back massage twice daily. I couldn't lift my little granddaughter without pain. I was missing out on so much.

Then St Thérèse came to Hampton Convent, Gracepark Road, and I went down on the Friday morning. We were ushered in and out very quickly. Then on Friday night, still in pain, I went back again. There was a vacant chair, and I sat down to pray and to listen to the readings and singing. It was a beautiful experience, and I asked St Thérèse to take my pain away; and she did.

It's now several weeks later, and I'm still free of the pain. I can do the garden and anything I want, and play with twenty-one-month-old Alex, and generally enjoy life now.

I think of and thank St Thérèse daily.

❦

BREDA BROWNE, KILKENNY

I am seventy-four years old and have been suffering from osteo-arthritis for about fifteen years. I used a wheelchair, walking aid, crutch and walking-stick — not for fifteen years, but for some time — and in the meantime I had a triple heart bypass in the Mater Hospital, Dublin, five years come December next.

When Thérèse came, my friend next door brought me the prayer, and she said it touched the casket; and ever since then I began feeling better. And then I saw Thérèse in Waterford shortly before she left Ireland. So now I am walking without any aid, or crutch or walking-stick.

So through St Thérèse I believe I am cured.

❦

ANONYMOUS, TIPPERARY

On Sunday, 24 June, having been unwell for some time, our nineteen-year-old daughter was urgently admitted to hospital Only a few days beforehand, we had discussed going to the sacred relics at Thurles Cathedral, should she be well enough to go on Monday, 25. Although she is a typical teenager, not really religious, I believe that, in agreeing to go, she opened the door for St Thérèse to enter her life.

Naturally, we were unable to go to Thurles the next night; but a friend was there who brought us a rose — a beautiful, very special rose; it simply brought tears to our eyes the moment we saw it. No other rose has ever had such an impact on my daughter, or me. It stayed perfectly fresh on her bedside locker for days. A firm phobia of needles and blood tests made life even more difficult for our patient, but even looking at the rose helped in some inexplicable way. Once, when having blood taken, a problem arose, and the nurse happened to remark on the rose. While she was trying for a vein, we told her how special it was; and suddenly all came right. She succeeded in taking the test. I shall always see her gloved hand tenderly touch the petals as she advised us to ask St Thérèse to help with a good result while she took it to the laboratory. Only a short time later she returned, to say [our daughter's] blood levels had improved that day.

Next came a man from our parish, also a patient, to give us his own relic and leaflet. Due to a renal problem, our daughter could not see properly, as her eyes were almost closed due to swelling. Having held the leaflet and read it, she suddenly exclaimed that she could now focus on the TV and also see clearly the bouquet of yellow chrysanthemums in the room which, prior to this, was a mere blur.

On learning that our girl needed to be transferred to a Dublin hospital, the kindly old hospital chaplain said, 'God is there too,' but the signs were few for some time in that busy secular world. However, in the worrying days during which we awaited a diagnosis, I continued to pray to the Sacred Heart of Jesus and St Thérèse.

Luckily I did manage a short visit to the reliquary at Mount St Joseph Abbey, Roscrea. Despite my tiredness and extreme distress at the illness of my daughter, I felt drawn to stay all night. The warmth of the sensation I experienced when I placed my hand on the casket will remain forever. An enormous sense of peace descended, and I had great hope that all would be well. Our prayer was for a definite diagnosis and that it would be treatable.

In a sports shop, of all places, I came across a *Buy and Sell*-type magazine. Among all the classified ads for cars, etc., was the short, three-day, unfailing prayer to the Sacred Heart. Of course I said it, and was rewarded within a few days.

Yes, we now know our daughter has Lupus SLE — an auto-immune disease, serious but treatable. With care, she will hopefully be able to live a normal life to a great extent. We believe St Thérèse simply 'moved in' and, hand in hand with the Sacred Heart, helped us all the way. We feel she was delegated by the Sacred Heart to help us in our time of need. Our daughter is now overwhelmingly devoted to her and has a special relationship with her. Being a young person too, surely St Thérèse can relate to all the worry and suffering which has come into her life, and helps her each day in so many ways.

❦

J. McC., ULSTER

I believe that I have been helped by the relic of St Thérèse. I had trouble with a sore on the side of my head for about two years — it would bleed if you knocked the top off — and it has completely healed; and so has the cysts which I had on my body, and I do not take any medication for a painful hernia, and I do not worry as much and feel closer to God.

❧

BERNADETTE O'SULLIVAN, KERRY

My name is Bernadette O'Sullivan. I am fourteen years old. All my life I have had problems gaining weight and height because of a problem with my stomach. I went to several different doctors but none knew what I could do. Then one day a friend of my mother's told me about a woman called Mary Buckley; I went to her, and she explained to me that I was allergic to gluten. Later Dr Leahy, paediatrician at Tralee General Hospital, ran some tests and said I was coeliac, which is a lifelong disease — no cure but a strict diet. I got used to having to ask people what was in foods. Most people did not know what it was and I had to explain every time.

I have always had a devotion to St Thérèse, so when I heard her relics were coming to Killarney on 19 June, I was delighted. I was determined to get there. When I did, people were selling roses to be blessed inside, but I never knew about buying one. But, as you probably already know, to ask for a prayer to be granted from St Thérèse is to say, 'Give me a rose'; and as I was walking in my aunt gave me a rose. We carried on walking in, and as we reached the casket I touched it and longed to stay longer, but we sat down for the Mass. Because I was a coeliac, I always had to take the Blessed Wine during Mass; but during this Mass I decided to take the Host, and afterwards I was glowing — my eyes were glistening and I felt very happy. After the Mass ended I felt perfect;

I was not sick at all. It was only now I thought about being given the rose.

And, thanks be to God and St Thérèse, I have been perfect since. I am now growing and gaining weight as normal. I am so grateful.

🌹

KITTY HENNESSY, DUBLIN

I had a ganglion on my finger for about two years. I was sent to Mr Colville in Beaumont Hospital. He said he would remove it.

On 10 May this year, I went to Mass in Clarendon Street and discovered St Thérèse was leaving after Mass. I went out and touched her casket and said farewell. I had already been to Hampton to see her.

Next day in Mass, I noticed I had no lump on my finger. I could not believe it, as I did not ask for anything. After Mass the hospital rang for me to go for the operation.

🌹

GERALDINE FORDE, CORK

I have to say, before I travelled to Kinsale with my husband I didn't have great faith in the saint — mainly because I didn't know a lot about her.

When we entered the church in Kinsale we were given a little prayer, which I rubbed on to the relic and then on to a wart on my face, which had been there for over six months. I had visited my doctor, who told me to have it surgically removed would leave a scar. I didn't do any more with it, and I used to pick it and it bled;

also, my face would get very hot. On the Monday morning, the wart was completely gone; and, up to this day, my face and skin are perfect. My husband also believes it. I have told many people I believe St Thérèse cured it; and, regardless of what anybody else thinks, I'm happy and cured.

❀

SHAUNA FORBES, TYRONE

My sister attended the cathedral in Derry when St Thérèse's relic visited Derry. She carried a bunch of red roses and brushed these across the relic. She gave each family member a blessed rose on her return.

My newborn baby girl had experienced a weepy left eye on leaving the hospital after her birth. The eye was watery and at times pus-y; it did not clear up with good hygiene, and I became concerned. I attended a local baby clinic, and they sent an eye swab for testing.

On return from the clinic, I put my faith in St Thérèse and blessed Lisa's eye three times with a blessed petal from my rose. The next morning, upon examination, her eye was clear — there was no water or pus. I put the healing down to St Thérèse's blessed petal.

When I phoned for the results of her eye swabs, a week later, I was told she had an infection which required antibiotic treatment. Fortunately I was able to tell them her eye was healed and all was well. Lisa's eye had been clean and clear ever since her overnight healing — a miracle in a way.

❀

JAMES MCGLYNN, LOUTH

When I was seven years of age, in the town of Wishaw in Scotland, I was playing with some of my friends. The year was 1927. We were crossing and re-crossing an old railway bridge over the disused lines, which had been closed a few years earlier. I slipped and fell about twenty-five to thirty feet onto the hard ground below, which was covered with old tin cans and broken bottles. My right arm was broken in three places.

I was taken to the Sick Children's Hospital, Yorkhill in Glasgow, which was sixteen miles from home. My condition became critical. Blood poisoning set into the wounds in my arm; the doctors tried to drain the poison from my arm, using glass tubes, to keep it from entering my system. The treatment was not working too well, so it was decided to remove my arm, to save further complications.

In the meantime, my mother, who travelled into Glasgow every day from Wishaw — which was pretty arduous for people at that time, coming by train and tram — met a very holy lady in our parish, which was St Ignatius in Wishaw. Her name was Lizzie O'Neil. Lizzie asked my mother how I was doing, and of course the news was not good. She gave my mother what she described as a relic of St Thérèse the Little Flower. When my mother visited the hospital that day, she tied the relic to my bed.

On the next morning, the doctors on their rounds noticed that there was an improvement in my condition, so they held off the surgery. My condition improved from then on, and no surgery was required. I was in hospital for twelve weeks; my arm was never back to normal, but I managed to get through life up to now. I believe it was through the intercession of St Thérèse that my arm was saved, and will always be grateful to her.

In fact, she may have saved me twice. When the Second World War broke out many of my friends had to go to war, but I was rejected for military service because I could not use my right arm to shoulder a gun.

When St Thérèse's relics came to Drogheda, I was happy to go to the Lourdes Auditorium to pay my respects to her.

❧

N.M. SMITH, ULSTER

I'm seventy-seven years old, and when I was eleven years I became very ill from St Vitus's Dance and rheumatic fever. My mother started a novena to the Little Flower on my behalf. Well, to make a long story short, I got well, and that was sixty years ago.

When the relics came to Derry, I went to visit the casket, as I was suffering violent pain from osteo and rheumatic spinal pain and needed to be on painkillers daily. Since touching the casket and praying at the time, I no longer need the painkillers, as I am without pain since.

Thank God and the Little Flower for my faith in St Thérèse for helping me twice in my lifetime.

❧

PEG MALLON, DUBLIN

In the past two years I have had two melanoma tumours removed from my legs, each one taking from six to eight months of daily dressing, etc., before they were completely cured. I don't have to say how I felt when I discovered yet another one just before I had to attend hospital to be discharged. The doctor, of course, diagnosed another tumour and said he would arrange to take a biopsy.

This was at the end of March. In the meantime, I just had to keep it covered to protect it against getting a knock. The biopsy was arranged for 28 June, and in the meantime my leg got worse and an ugly scab formed on it.

Then the Little Flower arrived in Rosslare, and the moment I heard of it I was convinced that she would cure it for me. I don't know why, because I never prayed to her, for the simple reason that long ago I heard that she always sent 'a thorn before the rose'. So I never would take the chance of that happening!

Anyway, when the reliquary came to Beaumont church I was taken up there, and was so carried away that all I could do was sit there while all around me people were praying fervently; all I did was say, 'Little Flower, show thy power, all for Jesus' sake.' That's all.

Then a strange thing happened. A lady came to my house — I think it was the following Friday; she had been to Hampton, and she handed me a picture of the Little Flower holding the roses. That did it. She had sent me the rose out of the blue, so I said, 'Now I know I'm going to be OK.'

I think my friend thought I was mad, because my leg was awful. Anyway, at some stage between then and the visit of the reliquary to Whitefriar Street, I changed the pad and the scab came with it, leaving nothing but a red patch on my leg. I went to Whitefriar Street, on my own, and all I could do was cry with gratitude.

The result of the biopsy came on 3 August and is completely clear. I must tell you that when I went to have the biopsy on 28 June, the doctor was taken aback, as there was nothing there; he said, 'This seems to have receded, but I'll do the biopsy just the same.'

All I know is, I'm cured. There's not even a mark to show the problem was ever there.

'My nature was such that fear made me recoil; with love
not only did I advance, I actually flew.'
Thérèse of Lisieux

Something Very Special

Interview with Pat Sweeney
Driver of the Thérèsemobile

Pat Sweeney: My devotion to St Thérèse started around 1978, when my wife Mary and I took our first holiday. We decided to go to Lisieux. Our eldest daughter, whom we named after St Thérèse, was about eight or nine years old at the time. I would have prayed to St Thérèse occasionally, but she didn't mean an awful lot to me at that stage.

When Father Linus Ryan came to Kildare, about ten years ago, I was introduced to him, and during the first year he asked me if I would like to go to Lisieux. No doubt, even then, I was starting to pick up certain vibes from St Thérèse. So I went to Lisieux that year, and since then I have totally fallen in love with Thérèse.

Father Ryan first introduced me to *Story of a Soul*. Initially I found it a little bit difficult to absorb. I was advised to read it a page at a time and try and take it in that way, so that's what I did. I have continuously prayed to St Thérèse since then. I pray to her every day. I learned her Act of Oblation off by heart so that when I am driving the car I can recite it. Every other time I just speak to Thérèse the same as I am speaking to you. If something goes wrong in my life, I will discuss it with Thérèse. If everything is going fine, I still discuss it with Thérèse. That may seem strange, but that's the way I communicate with her.

Don Mullan: When did the opportunity for driving the Thérèse-mobile come about?

PS: In 1999 I was asked if I would go on the Committee of the Theresian Trust, founded by Maurice Frost and his wife Christine, along with Father Ryan. When Maurice was dying he asked that I would replace him as Treasurer of the Trust.

I was very much involved, and so, when the relics were coming to Ireland, I felt very privileged. Again through Father Ryan, it was recommended I serve on the Steering Committee organising the visit.

My job initially was to look after the mail. To give you some idea of the amount, we had to hire a man to come and collect the mail from five different houses, and it took a truck to collect all the parcels and packages. At that time I wondered if the people would bother to read it.

But during the tour, at every venue, I saw the results. Who were the most prominent? The schoolchildren, thousands and thousands, lining the streets of Ireland, their teachers standing behind them. It was because they had been informed. They weren't left to pick it up from the papers and radio stations.

Through all the initial planning, my admiration for Father Ryan increased by the minute. There are no words can express it. I was the man who was closest to him during all of this. I have seen him work seventeen and eighteen hours a day. To ring me at twelve o'clock at night to ask me about something in the post wouldn't be unusual. As a matter of fact, if it didn't happen I would think there was something wrong.

I drove from Kildare to Terenure College one Saturday morning, and he told me to go to the dining-room and count the number of six-foot tables. There were sixteen. As I returned to his room I remember thinking, 'What have tables got to do with the relics?'

When I told him the number, he pointed to two bags filled with paper. He must have been up all night slicing open envelopes. He asked me to sort them out according to dates and venues. When this was done, we took a map of Ireland and looked at what dates were acceptable and what were not.

You can imagine the amount of work this took, involving all thirty-two counties. I was going around the tables for a couple of hours, putting down sheets of paper with the different venues followed by possible dates. I worked in operations in the Army, using a different method, but there was no question about it: I began to see it fall into place.

A Mercedes Sprinter was sponsored and modified to take the relics around Ireland. I volunteered to drive the vehicle. This was really something very special for me and, incidentally, it was too for my family, who were absolutely ecstatic because they felt that they would have chosen some professional guy who would be used to driving presidents. But no: Thérèse settled for a sergeant-major. As the journey began, the vehicle became popularly known as the 'Thérèsemobile' — I presume after the 'Popemobile' used to carry Pope John Paul II around Ireland in 1979.

Jim Doyle, my co-driver, helped me drive the Thérèsemobile in France. When we got to Ireland, Jim and I had an agreement: I was the main driver of the vehicle, and he and Liam O'Keeffe were co-drivers but with other responsibilities. Jim, who is a very close friend of mine, said to me, 'I'm quite happy to sit on board.' I would never have got through that trip without Jim Doyle. He was very important to me because he was the man who, when I got into a very tight spot, got out and gave guidance. As for Liam O'Keeffe, his good humour, gentleness and unstinting generosity in helping Father Ryan were extraordinary.

In the euphoria people rushed at the Thérèsemobile; they forgot about the small children in front of them, and you could find that a child might be very close to a back wheel. It was a 76hp turbo diesel engine, a very powerful vehicle, and the last thing I needed or wanted was an accident. It was very necessary to have Jim there to check all was well or to open the back doors. Jim also helped me to get the reliquary into place — a very important part of the job, as the casket weighed 480lbs.

I might also add that Father Ryan's comfort was very important; a special seat was put into the car because he has hip problems. How a man with ulcerated legs and problems with both hips could endure that journey is beyond me.

The Thérèsemobile was a marvellous vehicle; nothing else would have sufficed. We had three mobile phones on board; I had my own and Father Ryan had two. The numbers were released to the media and they were going all the time, every day.

DM: The criticism that was levelled towards the Army for carrying Thérèse — how did you feel?

PS: I joined the Army in 1963 and I served with the 40th Infantry Battalion overseas, the first Irish battalion to serve in the Mediterranean. A lot of people went to the Holy Land. What a lot of these people would want to realise is that we prided ourselves on being Catholic. I felt that when dignitaries come into this country they are afforded military honours. I personally wanted the Army involved for that reason.

Initially, on Easter Sunday morning when members of the 10th FCA Battalion marched onto the ship, the sergeant turned around and he marched over to me and he said they wanted permission to say a prayer before they had the honour of lifting the relics of St Thérèse. Now, I think that answers the question of whether these men wanted to do it. I felt it should be done, and I think the Army themselves certainly wouldn't have done it if they didn't want to do it. I think they saw it as a very important occasion. Our Army has been peacekeeping for the last forty years throughout the world, and why shouldn't they turn out for something like the visit of St Thérèse? The cynics — they don't bother me. I don't worry about them, because if it wasn't the Army they would find something else to talk about.

The Guards were the same; the Guards took this very personally. I know one Garda sergeant who told us, 'I'm supposed to be off duty, but I'm back in uniform. I wouldn't miss this for anything.' If you could see the enthusiasm — it was alive.

I have to say the RUC were brilliant also. They were very professional. They didn't force themselves into any situation. They took the job as it was. Some of them would wave or salute or just say hello; and if the man decided that he just didn't want to say anything, we respected him for his views. I would hold them in the same esteem as I would the Army and the Guards. Jim and I depended ultimately on all these people to get us to the venues, North and South. The RUC were very discreet in the way they did it: they avoided certain areas, respecting Protestant people who mightn't like to have the relics coming through their particular part of the town or something.

DM: Wasn't there one incident when you nearly got a parking ticket?

PS: While we were in Knock I took Bishop Patrick Ahern, the retired Auxiliary Bishop of New York, to meet his friend Monsignor Grealy. I parked the Thérèsemobile outside the presbytery, but there was a whole lot of 'No Parking' signs and beacons. I was after doing a complete crash course through the country on how to go through red lights with Guards bringing me through, so a 'No Parking' thing on the side of the road didn't mean anything to me.

After bringing Bishop Ahern into the presbytery I returned to the vehicle, and here was this big Garda with the book out and the pencil. I went up to him and he said, 'Are you the driver of this?' 'You mean the Thérèsemobile?' I asked, and he said, 'Yes.' I told him I was. 'Well,' he said, 'you are illegally parked. I'm giving you a ticket.'

I have to say that I knew the handcuffs could have been slapped on me and I could have been taken away; but, to be honest, I didn't care at that stage. 'You are a brave man,' I said. 'This car has certain privileges.' He said there were no privileges where illegal parking is concerned.

I said, 'This car has been escorted around Ireland by your fellow officers, and I have been shown nothing only the utmost respect. I believe in discipline and I am a law-abiding citizen, but I think you are pushing it just a little bit too far. Now, if you don't mind me making a suggestion to you, Guard, I think you should go down the other end of the town and stay down there till I'm gone!'

He did — he went off. Bishop Comiskey said to me, 'It's an awful pity you didn't let him stick it on, you know!'

DM: What are the most memorable moments of the eighty-eight days you had with Thérèse through Ireland and France?

PS: I would say that there are a few of them. Passing through Macroom, Co. Cork, and Glenties, Co. Donegal, it was like a national holiday: everything was closed and everybody was in the streets. I never saw such crowds of people on the entire journey; it was absolutely incredible. In Macroom there was a woman running at the side of the car. She shouted, 'Will you please, please stop? My child is very sick.' I told Jim to hop out and open the back doors. People rushed at the Thérèsemobile at this stage. I took the child up in my arms into the back — the child was unconscious — and I put the child lying down beside the reliquary. And I got a response from the child, but I didn't say anything to the mother because I didn't want to create any false hopes. To see a little child so sick and unconscious hit me very hard. It was very hard not to break down at the time.

Another one was in Spiddal, where a woman came to me and asked me if I would stop at her friend's house. She knew we would be passing her friend's house from checking the route with the Guards — the Guards and the Army were exceptional. I told the woman to be on the road; I told her she would have to wave to me in case I did not see her.

We were about three miles outside Spiddal, heading towards Galway, and I saw this woman frantically waving a paper. I stopped; I knew this was the house, so I got out and took a rose out of the back of the car and ran straight through the door. Her friend was in a wheelchair in the hallway. So I went in and I handed her the rose and I gave her a kiss, and I said, 'You couldn't come to see St Thérèse, but now she has come to see you.' She broke down and cried. To me that was an extra-special privilege because I was going into people's homes. Thérèse had planned everything, and we were only instruments.

The other one was down in Donncha Ó Dúlaing's hometown, in Doneraile. I saw a woman running along the side of the street and I thought she had two heads. She heard that the relics were coming and she picked up her sister, who had no use of her limbs, and she threw her over her shoulder. She was running along the road and from behind you would think she had two heads. I was actually going to stop as I got such a fright when I saw her.

When we got to the front of the church I saw her running back down the side of the road and there were beads of sweat on her. I said, 'My God, do you not have a wheelchair?' She said, 'No, I hadn't time. I thought I was going to miss the relics and it's very important for my sister.' I told her to sit down so we could get her a glass of water. I told her the Thérèsemobile was not leaving until she'd rested and her sister had time to venerate the relics. She was so grateful, because we did wait, and we brought her and her sister up and we let them venerate the relics by the side of the road.

Another memorable place, of course, was the North. The faith of those people! I cry now when I look at television and I see the terrible pain that they must be going through, all at the hands of a few people who just don't want to see peace. I am a witness, having driven up the Ardoyne to see the houses, all with bunting or a picture of St Thérèse, and those people were kneeling in the streets; they weren't standing, they were kneeling in the streets.

A very special personal memory was visiting my wife Mary's hometown of Ballybay, Co. Monaghan. We owe a debt of gratitude to Monsignor McSorley and Teresa Connolly, who helped organise a massive turnout of the people.

The rest of the venues in Ireland were all fabulous in their own ways, and they all had their own stories to tell. To drive the relics into my own hometown was a dream come true.

My favourite bishops were John Magee and Brendan Comiskey. I was very taken by Bishop Magee, not because he was secretary to three popes but because he was a man who made us feel that what we had done was very important to him and to his people. He walked us around the cathedral grounds; we stopped and we talked, and we admired the beautiful view over the harbour in Cobh. All the bishops treated us with the utmost respect. I felt, however, one bishop was very unfair to us because we arrived late at his cathedral. I was astounded by his rudeness. We were driving the relics of this wonderful saint — the greatest saint of modern times — and the man wasn't switched on. How could we pass any sick child or invalid? What priest or bishop would mind waiting an hour if he thought you were bringing that sort of comfort and joy to people less fortunate than ourselves?

Irish Ferries were fabulous. They hosted us out and coming back. They had a special room set up for the reliquary and a Master-at-Arms guarding it from the time it was on board. Madeline O'Shaughnessy of Irish Ferries was a beautiful person. She was an absolute lady to deal with.

If you think of all the Carmelite houses and the convents, it was an exceptional time for the nuns themselves, because the nuns can't leave; they can't come out and get on a plane and go to Lisieux the same as priests can.

Then there's the story of the helicopter pilot flying from Waterford to Lough Derg. Just before the helicopter took off, the weather report was that storms were brewing and that it was very dicey. There was the possibility that the helicopter might have to turn back or land along the route.

The pilot, who is from Bristol, told me that when he lifted up, the clouds parted, and that there was a blue streak heading the whole way in the direction of Lough Derg. He said to me, 'I could see the storm on both sides but we had a clear passage the whole way to Lough Derg. Let me tell you,' he continued, 'I wouldn't mind carrying this lady every day of the week.' It was the same thing coming back.

It was the greatest privilege of my life. At times, on the trip, everybody, to be very truthful, would have gotten on each other's nerves from time to time. I said to Father Ryan, 'You know, one of the little miracles, one of the roses, is the fact that the four of us are still speaking to one another.' And that was a very human thing, you know. We would have a meal in the evening, sit down, talk about the day and what had happened and discuss a lot of things.

❧

'... *it seems to me that the darkness, borrowing the voice of sinners, says mockingly to me: "You are dreaming about the light....* *Advance, advance; rejoice in death which will give you not what you hope for but a night still more profound, the night of nothingness."'*

Thérèse of Lisieux

❧

'I felt that I was loved … it was no longer simply a look, it was a fusion; they were no longer two, Thérèse had vanished as a drop of water is lost in the immensity of the ocean.'
Thérèse of Lisieux

4

A Great Comfort

FATHER GERARD MCCLOSKEY, ANTRIM
(organiser of the Belfast visit)

It was half-past one when Father Frank — one of the Carmelites who was looking after the mobile shop — came up to me:

'Father Gerry, there are two ladies complaining that the mobile library is blocking the view from their house. Will you go and talk to them?'

The relics were due in half an hour's time. I was up to my neck ensuring that everything was running smoothly. I kept my cool and went over to the two ladies.

'That van is blocking our view!' they told me. I had arranged for the mobile shop to be situated there. It was the perfect place, right in front of St Peter's Cathedral! Without showing my annoyance, I talked to them. Seeing that they were very determined to have the van moved, I thought it wiser to keep calm and to accede to their request.

Six weeks later, I received a phone call from a young lady in the parish asking me to give a blessing to her sick uncle, who, she told me, was a good and upstanding Protestant. She told me that he was at death's door and that he had asked for a priest.

As I arrived at the house, I could see two ladies standing in the conservatory. One of them disappeared very quickly.

'Father, my aunt has to run to the back of the house because she gave you a hard time the day of the relics.'

'What hard time did she give me?' I enquired.

'She made you move the van!'

Suddenly I remembered the incident.

'Come on out, little flower!' I said, deliberately putting everyone at their ease.

The lady introduced me to her sister. 'Father, this is Rose, and her husband Sammy is dying with cancer: the doctor has given him less than a week.'

'And you want me to give him a blessing?'

'No, Father,' Rose interjected, 'I want you to marry us!'

Rose went on to explain to me that she came from the Falls and Sammy came from the Shankill. Over forty years previously, she and Sammy had been going out together and wanted to get married. There were difficulties in Rose's home, and so they arranged in the space of a few days to get married in the Church of Ireland at the bottom of the Shankill Road. This meant that Rose could no longer receive the Sacraments, having married without the permission of her Church. She told me that this was something that she had always regretted, and that Sammy had been as intent as she was to get it sorted out from the Catholic side. In all those years, Rose had never lost her faith. In particular she had a great devotion to the Little Flower. She had passed on that devotion to Sammy and to a lot of their Protestant friends.

'The night before the relics were due in Belfast,' she told me, 'I brought Sammy over to stay in my sister's house, seeing as it is situated right outside St Peter's Cathedral.'

I was so glad that I had kept my cool that day. 'No wonder they wanted to have the van moved,' I thought to myself.

I telephoned the Bishop and received all the necessary permissions. I went into Sammy's bedroom to meet him. Everything I had been told about him was true. He was a real gentleman. As Sammy and Rose exchanged vows and had their wedding rings blessed, I noticed a statue of the Little Flower at his bedside with a lighted candle in front of it.

'Now, Rose,' Sammy whispered to her, 'our Little Flower in Heaven has got us our request, and I am going up there to join her.'

Sammy died peacefully three days later.

❦

JOSEPH MCKENNA, ANTRIM

On 28 February 2001 I had an accident to my right eye: a piece of metal pierced my eye and lodged at the back of the eye. I went to hospital and was told I would require major surgery, which would involve inserting an artificial lens after the metal had been removed.

After the surgery, the vision in my eye was very blurred. My medication was eye-drops for six weeks; after the six weeks I visited the eye specialist, and he told me I was allergic to the drops, which had stained my eye, resulting in a deterioration of the vision in my eye. I was taken back to hospital for further surgery, but an infection was discovered at the back of my eye and the operation had to be abandoned.

During all this time I had been praying to St Thérèse; also I had been to Knock and got a novena to St Thérèse, which my wife and I say every day.

On my next visit to hospital, I was told I would require further surgery, as scar tissue had developed at the site of the infection. My specialist advised me that he would seek another opinion as to the possibility of turning the cornea, as the scar tissue was affecting my vision.

At this time the relics of St Thérèse had arrived in Belfast, and my wife and I went to St Peter's Cathedral. While waiting outside the cathedral, as there were very large crowds, I looked up and was able to read a banner over the church door with my injured eye, very plain. This was the best vision I had in my eye since before the accident. When we entered the cathedral, my vision was much improved. After I had venerated the relics, I received a great comfort and strength.

On my next visit to hospital I was told [by the specialist] that my eye was much improved, as the scar tissue was fading, and further surgery would not be required. He was very pleased with the progress of my eye.

I have been able to drive again and return to work, and my sight continues to improve. We continue to pray to St Thérèse every day, and we know that it is through her help that I am at this stage now.

❧

NOLEEN CONNELL, MEATH

I am an eighteen-year-old girl who was in an accident at work in March of this year, which left me with two broken wrists, a fracture to the base of my skull, deafness in my left ear and paralysis of the fifth nerve on the left side.

I began to see doctors in Beaumont Hospital. All they could tell me is that it would take time — the doctors didn't say exactly how long, but it could take up to a year or more. So a month or so passed; I tried a few different things — a rub, steroids — and no definite improvement.

My mother mentioned St Thérèse was coming to Drogheda on a Sunday night. I must admit I was a bit doubtful about going, but at that stage I would have tried anything.

On Tuesday of that week I noticed a change in my eye: it wasn't sore, and I didn't have to use my drops. The paralysis in my face gradually got better over the following weeks. Recently, when I went for a check-up in Beaumont, they noticed a good improvement in my hearing and my face, which surprised them.

When I heard St Thérèse was coming to Stamullen, Co. Meath, I again visited her in thanksgiving.

❦

LELIA CONSIDINE, TIPPERARY

Last January my sister's husband's speech became slurred; following investigations, he was diagnosed with Motor Neurone Disease. Needless to say, my sister, their children and extended family were and are devastated with this news. Jim has been a very special member of our family for thirty-five years. His illness has progressed rapidly. He is now, six months later, almost at wheelchair stage.

Before the visit to Ireland of St Thérèse's relic, my sister was given a prayer to say to St Thérèse. On the Monday we were in

Limerick, and my sister decided to go to St John's on Monday night to make a vigil during the visit of the relics, which she did from 1.00 to 5.00 a.m. Next day we were told that the 'Relicmobile' had pulled into their gateway en route to Limerick earlier on Monday — unknown to us, St Thérèse visited Jim, who was in his house unable to travel to any of the churches where Thérèse was. (We think the Thérèsemobile was waiting for the escort into Limerick.)

The family's prayers have been for acceptance of this illness. While the illness is progressing at an alarming rate, everyone is coping a little better, thank God, and Jim is in good form despite the disabilities of his disease.

A lady in the nursing home has had a very bad leg ulcer for nine months. Visits to hospital and specialist care appeared to fail to heal this ulcer. I put a petal from the roses I bought in Thurles and touched off the casket into the dressing. The leg is now almost healed, and I am thrilled; it was very painful, and we were very worried as we felt it would never heal. Was it St Thérèse? I'd like to think so!

❧

SISTER IMMACULATA, DUBLIN

There were two men hereabouts who had fallen out and had not spoken to each other for many years. The first evening the relics were here, the wife of one of them suggested to her husband that they come up and visit them. He demurred, said he'd wait till the next day when the crowds would have eased off. However, she persisted and finally managed to persuade him to come, albeit under protest. As they were walking up the avenue, who should

they see coming down from the chapel but the other man. Simul-
taneously both men approached one another with outstretched
hands, and a warm handshake cancelled the years of estrangement
and consigned all the rancour to the past. St Thérèse had made
them friends once more.

🌹

H.P.K., DUBLIN

As one of those who were spiritually touched by the occasion of the
visit of the sacred relics of St Thérèse of Lisieux, may I say that up to
this time I did not give any special attention to the saint. However,
for some reason unknown to myself, when I read about the
proposed visit of the saint's relics I felt jerked into a special interest,
and when my wife asked me to drive her to attend the veneration
in Grace Park Road, Drumcondra, I felt this was a special call which
I grasped at. To my surprise, she asked me again the next day to
make a second visit, which we did.

I may mention that I had a heart attack about six months
previously and was not feeling the best, but almost from the time I
made the visits to the saint's relics I began to feel much improved
and more energetic. I am not claiming a miracle, but the improvement in my health and energy has continued to increase, and I find
myself saying prayers daily, asking for the intercession of Saint
Thérèse.

It is true for me to say that I was touched by the visit of the saint's
relics, and while I am not over-religious I feel she has greatly influenced my spiritual outlook. I feel grateful for the spiritual impact she
has brought to me.

🌹

ANNE, CLARE

After visiting St Thérèse, an upsetting disagreement was settled that I never thought was possible.

🌹

FLORENCE MAHONY, GALWAY

The most poignant memory I have of St Thérèse's visit to Loughrea is of a young couple, Michelle and Mark, who came to venerate the reliquary and brought their little baby girl, Christina, who was only a few months old and very ill. They spent an hour praying with St Thérèse, during which a stranger came over to Michelle and handed her a rose for Christina. Both Michelle and Mark were very moved and brought it home and dried it.

Christina got very ill and was taken to Crumlin Hospital. Her parents decided to get her the Sacrament of Confirmation, and they gave her 'Thérèse' as her confirmation name. When she was confirmed, she had the rose that was given to her in the pocket of her dress.

Sadly, Christina died shortly afterwards. Michelle and Mark are going through very difficult times — Christina was their first-born baby — but the visit of the reliquary helped them.

Another local person, Mary, who was suffering from cancer, had great devotion to St Thérèse. She was very excited about the visit, and she came to pray with Thérèse every day. She came to St Brendan's Cathedral on Thursday, to say farewell to her true friend, and she got a bad turn and was brought home. Her loving daughter, Maura, told me that her mum asked her that day to let her go to her place of rest, that she was ready to go and could not fight her illness any longer. During her last few days she prayed for all the people who had lost the faith, that they would convert back to prayer. On 19 June, she died at her home with her family around her. At her funeral Mass her son, Father Frank, spoke of a tremendous smell of roses that filled the room shortly after his mother Mary died.

Thérèse's visit to my lovely town of Loughrea will always remain deep in my heart.

❧

V. McD., DUBLIN

I am happy to say I have been helped by St Thérèse of Lisieux.

I'm an elderly lady and needed serious surgery early last year. I prayed to Thérèse and she listened and heard my plea; I had no complications, thank God, and I'm recovering rapidly. At the same time, quite a large cheque came my way very unexpectedly. It was at the time very badly needed for medical treatment for a close relative. She was really happy to benefit from the miracle.

I just want to say that I find it difficult to put into words how strongly I felt the help of the Little Flower, in each case sending yellow roses as a gift, which I was not aware of until afterwards. Then it confirmed my thoughts, if confirmation was needed.

I always had the feeling that St Thérèse would change the minds of the youth of Ireland and I hope she has. I really did not think I would be personally touched by her powers. Now I know I have, and I will be forever grateful for the graces and pray to her daily.

❦

SISTER FINIAN HEGARTY, DONEGAL

[I was recently] diagnosed as having dystonia, a chronic neuro-
logical disorder. The underlying cause of dystonia is not clear —
abnormality in the basal ganglia, an area deep within the brain
whose function is to co-ordinate the movement of the muscles. It is
only recently my GP had some information about dystonia. He then
suggested I see a neurologist.

The trouble then started, trying to get a quick appointment. The
first one was November and this was 13 March. The next one was
27 June.

At this time I was suffering very severe pain, and my head and
neck kept turning to the left-hand side. I was in such pain and
unable to sleep.

Then came the moment I implored the help of Thérèse of
Lisieux. I kept praying to her day and night. I knew the relics were
coming to the cathedral [in Derry]. Feeling so sick and weak, I
thought I would never make it. One of the Sisters came to me and
told me she would come with me on the bus.

We arrived at the cathedral shortly before the relics. I felt a great
peace as I walked towards the relics; as I prayed the prayer to
St Thérèse, I knew my prayers would be answered. It was indeed a
sight to behold in Derry's cathedral that night. That was a
Wednesday.

I began the prayer to St Thérèse on the day the relics arrived at
St James's Hospital, and on the day after I finished the novena my
appointment card arrived — which was also a Wednesday, and it
was for just two weeks away, which was 15 May. I was so delighted.

Had I waited until 27 June, I would have missed the wedding of my niece on 27 June and the death of my very loved ninety-three-year-old aunt who died on 27 June. I was at the bedside as she made her journey into Heaven. That was also a Wednesday.

On 15 May (Wednesday) I got my first two injections of botulism toxin, and within four days I felt a great improvement. As the neurologist could only give me a small amount, he told me it would help for a few weeks, which it did. I feel it coming back a little, but not as severe. Thérèse of Lisieux has heard my prayer.

❦

ANNETTE CUMMINS, KILKENNY

In 1963, my sister Teresa was dying of cancer and she was being cared for at home. She and I had both just finished our training as nurses. A few weeks before she died, I read a book someone had left about St Thérèse. I forgot about it then until, on the day our Teresa died, I had laid her out upstairs and then gone down. After a while, with a very heavy heart, I thought how would I go up to the room again. Just as I began to climb the stairs, I got a most beautiful smell of perfume, and at the same time I felt my feet were off the ground and I could have flown up. The lovely scent surrounded me while I walked up and around the room, and then went.

The experience helped me to bear the pain of loss of a loved one at the time. I know St Thérèse helped me.

❦

ANGELA O'ROURKE, WATERFORD

Presently I am being treated for bone cancer. I hadn't been able to eat, lost weight and was unable to tolerate my treatment; my quality of life was very poor. Tea and cornflakes was my staple diet. A friend took me to Tallow Carmelite monastery on Sunday, 17 June. I spent two hours at the casket with no interest whatsoever. As I got up to leave I said to St Thérèse, 'I don't want anything from you except the coping skills to deal with my situation.'

I never looked back since. My treatment is suiting me, my strength has come back and my appetite is unbelievable.

I attended four venues and saw her off from Wexford Park. What a memorable day and time! St Thérèse did something very special for me, as I was physically, mentally and spiritually broken; like St Thérèse, I experienced the absence of God in my life.

❦

MARCE, DUBLIN

I firmly believe that St Thérèse changed my life for the better. I heard her remains were coming to Ireland, long before she arrived. I immediately thought, 'I will visit, no matter where I have to travel.' By the way, I am not a very religious person; but, for some unknown reason, I wanted to visit St Thérèse's relic.

I went to the Carmelite monastery in Drumcondra. I did not feel anything there, but all through the night I kept wakening and thinking about her. I began to say her novena and asked very special requests from her. The requests were granted and therefore changed my life completely.

Some weeks later I got a call for a mammogram. I had pain in my left breast. I got the all-clear. I was then called back for a second screening: they found something on the right breast. I had a mammogram and was then taken for an ultrasound. Up until then I was a thirty-to-forty-per-day cigarette smoker. While I was waiting my turn for the ultrasound, I made a promise to St Thérèse that if I got the all-clear, I would never smoke again as long as I live, no matter what happens to me in my lifetime. I know I can do it, because it is little enough in return for what she has done for me. I also promised I would visit her relic as much as I could. I went to three other parishes also. I carry her relic and her novena everywhere. I love St Thérèse so very much, and I am very grateful to her for all she has done for me.

🌹

MRS KATHLEEN DELANEY, KILKENNY

My story about St Thérèse begins some weeks before her relics arrived in Ireland, when I came across a little prayer to her. As my husband Jerry and I, both elderly, do the Stations of the Cross and say the Rosary around three o'clock every afternoon, we then included St Thérèse's prayer.

On Palm Sunday, the Sunday before Easter, I got word from my nephews that my younger sister Anne, their mother, had collapsed on her way to hospital. She was in a coma and brain-damaged. So I was upset all that week.

On Holy Saturday, Jerry and I decided to go to St Mary's Cathedral to go over the Stations. I was never a follower of St Thérèse until I got the prayer, but before the Stations I decided to go to St Thérèse's statue and said, 'St Thérèse of the Child Jesus, remember your promise to do good on earth. Shower down your roses on all who invoke you. Ask Our Lord if it is His holy will to take Anne out of this world because of her present circumstances.'

We went to the church at 12.45 p.m. and came out at 1.05 p.m. We got a phone call during that day to say Anne had passed away at 1.00 p.m.

❀

ALICE, DUBLIN, AND PETER, MOUNTJOY PRISON

Alice: My own memories pale into insignificance when I read an account of a foster son's visit to the relics at Mountjoy Prison. Peter had been on drugs and ended up in prison because he stole to feed his habit, like most drug users.

Peter: St Thérèse honoured us yesterday with her company. I really enjoyed the ceremony and it made me feel how lucky I was to be in her presence. I will more than likely never in my time on Earth be in the same room as a saint again. A priest from the Carmelites in Stillorgan came to give a small talk and explain a bit about St Thérèse. I do believe St Thérèse wanted to come to places that were usually forgotten. I think she was very happy yesterday, and that rubbed off on me.

❀

MARY, TIPPERARY

[When St Thérèse's relics visited Thurles,] the moment I went into the cathedral, in the small hours of the morning, I felt this inner peace and it was a lovely feeling. When I looked around I could not believe all the young people that were there with smiles on their faces, and no one in a rush.

At that time I was on the mend from my depression, but from that night on I handled it in a different way. When I feel a bit down now, some little thing clicks in and reminds me of the positive side of my life — a wonderful husband and family. I find it hard to explain, but I do know that it's all down to St Thérèse.

I could have sat there all night in the church, but my husband had work next morning so we had to leave. It was a night I will never forget, and I can honestly say it has changed my life for the better. I can still see the hundreds of candles flickering all over the church. For some strange reason it makes me cry, but with joy, not sadness.

I have learned to focus on the good things, not dwell in the past, and it's a great feeling. I took in my own rose from my garden and had it blessed; then I dried the petals between the pages of a book, and I am going to put them in a frame so that I will always have them.

'... the only good is to love God with all one's heart and
to be poor in spirit here on earth.'
Thérèse of Lisieux

5

'I Know It's a Miracle'

ANONYMOUS

I visited the relics of St Thérèse at two locations, Dublin and Knock. I have been aware of St Thérèse all my life but couldn't say I have particular devotion to her. However, I was drawn to visit her relics because of a sense of the faith of ordinary people.

Directly after visiting the relics, I became pregnant. This was deemed medically impossible for us, so I consider this a miracle. I attribute this miracle to the intercession of St Thérèse.

MARIE DOYLE, DUBLIN

In January of this year I was diagnosed with having a cancerous ovarian tumour. During my period of receiving chemotherapy, I went to visit the relics of St Thérèse on 2 May in the Carmelite convent in Malahide, Co. Dublin, along with my sister. On my return to my doctor, he was amazed to tell me that the cancer had been treated — which he honestly said he had not expected initially — and that, in some ways, he felt it was a miracle. He had never seen the like of it before. He then proceeded to operate on me again and was amazed that the tumour had actually shrunk.

❧

ANONYMOUS, DONEGAL

First and foremost, I would like to say that for the past twelve years I have had a great devotion to St Martha, whose intercession has yielded me miraculous favours. However, in the past three years St Thérèse has proved as wonderful a friend as St Martha.

Shortly before Christmas 1998, my GP requested an ultrasound scan on my gall bladder. The symptoms appeared trivial; but on examination the radiologist detected something in my pancreas, which a CT scan showed to be a malignant tumour. I was devastated.

Within days, many novenas and prayers poured into our home — and among them the story of and prayer to St Thérèse. I began a daily novena to her. Within a week there was some amazing happenings. A very close friend arrived with a bunch of yellow roses, which she picked up by chance in the florist's. Then, at Christmas, with the ground covered in snow, a rosebush in our garden was covered with yellow roses. At that moment I was convinced I would survive this killer disease.

When I heard of the relic of St Thérèse coming to Ireland, I was very excited and made plans to visit the sacred relics in Derry, only to discover that we would be on holiday at that time. Imagine my delight, on a visit to Drogheda during May, to discover the sacred relics were there. I was among a party who went to the church at 11.30 p.m. Having spent some time there in prayer, we headed back to the car.

Suddenly there was a smell of roses all around me. Then one of my friends said, 'Smell the roses.' Six of us stood there in wonder. There was no flowers or roses anywhere in the vicinity.

In July I went to Lourdes as a working nurse with the Derry Diocesan Pilgrimage. One day, as we were leaving the underground basilica, I was overwhelmed with the scent of roses. On looking up, there was a large portrait of St Thérèse, and those wonderful eyes piercing into our very souls. I felt such utter peace.

It will be three years in December since I was diagnosed with pancreatic cancer. The first miracle: it was found at a very early stage without spread. The second miracle: I survived toxic poisoning caused by an overdose of chemotherapy — only three per cent of people survive toxic poisoning. In May 2001 my CT scans were clear, and my next check-up is in May 2002.

I thank God and his saints every day for such good health. I feel as healthy as I ever did; but still I have the odd doubt. On these occasions, someone will present me with a yellow rose.

❦

EILEEN FORDE, MEATH

I am a widow aged seventy-seven years. Five years ago I was diagnosed with fibrotic lung disease, increasingly getting worse. I am depending on oxygen all night, and to walk outside my home I needed portable oxygen. I wear tracheotomy tubes, I have high blood pressure, heart failure and diabetes.

When St Thérèse's relics was in Mullingar, I had some problems getting my invalid daughter — age thirty-five, confined to a wheelchair and in a nursing home in Kells — to Mullingar. She is waiting on major surgery in her stomach. I was interceding for her safe recovery. It was very emotional, touching Thérèse's casket with our roses. Since then I have dried the petals and shared them out.

My experience since then is I feel I have got a new lease of life. My energy has come back, and I am well able to do housework that was impossible before the visit. I am also able to walk around my house and up the garden without oxygen. I say her novena and bless myself with the rose petals daily, but my prayers are for my daughter and my son who is waiting on an operation on his eye following an accident. He has lost the sight. I will continue to ask her help and thank her for all she has done for me. My family can't believe the improvement. I know it's a miracle.

❧

MAURA CATHCART, FERMANAGH

It was Monday, 21 May 2001. The bones of St Thérèse were arriving at Cavan Cathedral. We had planned to go late that night to see them.

Dad had been admitted to the Erne Hospital, Enniskillen, on Sunday, 20 May 2001 with — as we thought — flu. He had been unwell all that previous week and had been very weak and off his food. The doctor visited him on two occasions and was called again on Sunday morning. It was then that Dad agreed to go to hospital. He walked onto the ambulance at home and was in reasonably good form and said 'cheerio' to the family. We were going to the hospital after the ambulance.

When we arrived at the hospital, we certainly were not expecting what was facing us. Dad was in bed and was complaining of not being able to see and was very confused. Mum knew straight away that something was after happening to him. Her worst fear was now a reality: Dad had taken a stroke.

He was immediately rushed to ICU and his condition deteriorated rapidly. A doctor confirmed to us that he had taken a stroke, possibly on his way to hospital. At this stage Dad was very confused, couldn't see and was very agitated. We were told that if his eyesight did not return within the next twenty-four hours, then the possibility of it returning was very slim. We were devastated. We sat with him throughout the night.

The next day, Monday, 21 May 2001, the family was called for and things looked very grim indeed. There was no light at the end of the tunnel at all. Later on that afternoon Dr Kelly, who specialises in stroke patients, examined Dad. He told us the news was not good. Dad had taken a brain-stem stroke, which is the worst type of stroke that one can take. It meant that his speech, sight and swallow were affected. They couldn't rule out the possibility of another stroke, which would kill him. The next forty-eight hours were crucial. If he was lucky enough to live, then there was a very, very high chance of total blindness.

All that day we were praying for a miracle. Various priests visited Dad and blessed him, and numerous Masses were said for him. We were aware that St Thérèse was in Cavan that day and we were praying earnestly to her to cure him.

By later evening of that day Dad took a turn. His blood pressure and blood level had dropped. He looked dreadful and he was very weak. We started praying and saying the Rosary at his bedside. Suddenly our aunt-in-law, Teresa, who came from seeing St Thérèse's bones in Cavan, reached over us and put a rose and

St Thérèse's relic on Dad's bed. It was then we knew he would recover. St Thérèse was with him and us.

Dad had a bad night that night and was very low about 4.00 that morning. Miraculously, the next day there was a slight improvement in his condition and also in his sight, even though he himself never knew he lost it. By evening-time his sight had partially returned, and by the next day it was completely back. Dad was moved out of ICU on Wednesday, and on Thursday he was moved to the Stroke Rehabilitation Unit, where he remained, convalescing, for three and a half weeks. He is now back home and is progressing and getting stronger every day.

We attribute this miraculous recovery to St Thérèse. Later, when we were speaking to the doctor, we were thanking him and his staff for all they had done for Dad, and he replied, 'Don't thank us; someone up there was looking after him.' Any of the nurses who cared for Dad when he was very ill in ICU couldn't believe his rapid recovery and called him 'the Miracle Man'.

Thank you, St Thérèse.

*'I was in love with the wide open spaces. Space and the
gigantic fir tress, the branches sweeping down to the ground,
left in my heart an impression similar to the one I experience
still today at the sight of nature.'*

Thérèse of Lisieux

'There are things the heart feels but which the tongue and
even the mind cannot express.'
Thérèse of Lisieux

6

Deep, Heartfelt Prayer

❧

AGNES CARLEY, ROSCOMMON

When at last the reliquary arrived in Longford, the attention to detail, sense of reverence, local support, tasteful decorations and huge attending numbers marked its lying in state in front of the high altar in St Mel's Cathedral. There was an evident aura of warmth and well-being everywhere in its precincts. Crowds filed slowly past the reliquary, and what really impressed me was the devotion and loving tenderness with which people of all ages and abilities filed through, sometimes lingering as if to wrench the last vestige of comfort and grace from the occasion.

On arriving home around midnight, my daughter announced she was going over to Longford, asking if I'd accompany her — hence my return journey. In the quietness of the cathedral we sat in the front seat, immediately behind the reliquary, soaking in the atmosphere and marvelling at the fact that we were in the presence of such holiness. I will always cherish those few hours as among the nicest and most faithful of my life. I regained the ability of deep, heartfelt prayer which I'd feared had forsaken me. When growing up, I inherited a deep-seated faith from parents whose trust in God was unfaltering. Modern attitudes had eroded that great trust which had been such a part of my life. The grace of St Thérèse's visit strengthened my prayer ability and I find, since then, that I can pray with a depth of devotion and earnestness that had, for some time, been eluding me. That, for me, is the great testimony of her visit.

❦

BETTY COOKE, LIMERICK

When I was very young I always prayed to Thérèse, especially because of her ill health, as I was frail enough growing up — thank God, I improved greatly. Thérèse always interceded for me and kept me close to Jesus and protected me. The visit of her relic was like the icing on the cake or a dessert after a meal — to have her so near, and just to thank her for my deep faith and love of God, and just take in her presence, as she is full of the love of God.

When Thérèse's relic came to the cathedral in Limerick, my husband dropped myself and my eight-year-old off at the cathedral at 8.00 p.m. because my son wanted to say hello to Thérèse and thank her for telling us about God's love. I was happy enough looking in the main door outside the big gate, and I could feel her presence all around, and everyone was so pleasant and courteous.

The church was full for Mass and the queue had built up. At about 9.15 I said to my little boy, 'Thérèse will have to work a miracle for us, otherwise we'll have to try and get home,' because the queue had only begun to move. He was so disappointed. And lo and behold, as I walked away I met a priest friend and he said, 'Have you been in yet?' and I said, 'No.' So he just said, 'Follow me,' and before I knew it I was beside the casket.

I touched the casket and then sat there in a nearby seat. My son kept going over to Thérèse's relic, at every side of it; he even got a rose for my sister, who has Parkinson's. The peace and spirituality that I experienced was too wonderful for words. I thought of Thérèse's words, that God was a God who saves, not a God who judges. My little boy said, 'I had a word in Thérèse's ear for you,' because I had been a bit tired.

There in the church, I seemed to be caught up in a dialogue with Thérèse; it was as if all that I learnt about the good Lord and herself surged up in my soul. It was like as if she was saying, 'Go out into the world and proclaim the good news to all creation.' I remember one time I read a bit about a rose, and this is what it said: 'The spread of Christianity could be compared to the rose.' It said the rose just spreads its fragrance, it doesn't have to say anything; so in Christianity, no need to preach — it is rather about drawing people into this beautiful aroma. And it was all around me as I sat there in her presence; I felt that draw to Christ. She is always directing us to Jesus.

What does success matter? What God asks of us is not to stop from the fatigue of the struggle, not to become discouraged. We must do our duty to the end. Her fiery love is first and foremost a work of grace — which is what is to be admired in Thérèse, rather than Thérèse herself.

The reason St Thérèse's visit touched so many people was because of all the prayer that was put into the preparation before she arrived and before she came to each county or cathedral. The Holy Spirit was so alive during her visit, it was electric, tangible; it was like a piece of dynamite. And this is what the Holy Spirit does — it just takes someone or something to awaken it in us.

Our mission is to keep our hearts open to the Gospel message, now that Thérèse has the groundwork done. We have to sow the seeds and nurture them so that they may blossom to fruition. Let's keep it going — a whole nation moving in God's power and grace. As Thérèse says, the time is now, the present moment.

❦

MICHAEL COOKE (AGED 8), LIMERICK

I love Thérèse. She is a great friend. I prayed for a girl that it was God's will she'd get a job and she did. Thérèse helps me a lot when I put a word in her ear at Mass. I will pray to her and ask her for peace in Ireland and for those who do not know Jesus that they will find him.

I liked going to the relic and I didn't mind being there for a long time and I liked talking to her in my prayers. I remembered about Thérèse in the missions and that Thérèse wanted to be a nun. I want to be a priest and people say that I am too young, but I pray to St Thérèse because she never changed her mind. I missed the relic going but I remembered about her spirit.

Thérèse, thanks for telling us all about the love Jesus has for us. Thanks for coming to Ireland. I like the story where you go fishing with your daddy, Thérèse. I love you very much.

❦

COLMAN, LONDON

Two years ago I was working in [London] at Holborn Underground Station. I did not like the job; it was very hard work. I wanted to be moved to another job as soon as possible. Then one day, on my dinner break, I went to the bank to get some money; on my way back I was passing a Catholic church. I went inside and there was a statue of St Thérèse of Lisieux. I went down on my knees to her to get moved from the job that I was on at the station. I went to light a candle to her. One week later I was sent to another job, where I made a lot of money. In eighteen months that money bought me a house in Co. Kerry.

I now go to Mass every Sunday. She is indeed a truly great saint.

❧

BETTY DILLON, LIMERICK

I saw the relics on television arriving in Rosslare and again watched them as they went to the different places throughout the country, and hadn't the remotest interest and wasn't in the slightest moved and had very little inclination, if any, of going to see them when they would come to Limerick. After their departure from Knock, my sister, who is a Carmelite nun there, rang me specially (something she rarely does) to expound on the wonderful privilege 'twas to have had the relics, on how touched she was and on how much God loves us. She was so euphoric. Again I barely listened, thinking all the time of the Limerick hurlers and how far they would go in this year's championship. However, her parting words to me were, 'They [the relics] are not to be missed.' For some reason that stuck, and after that 'twas nagging at me that I should go to see them.

Now this would be a difficult task enough, as my husband has lost an eye and I have a leg problem which would make either walking or standing very uncomfortable and would rule out driving through the city for my husband. The relics arrived in St John's Cathedral, Limerick, on a Monday and I decided that at 5.30 a.m. Tuesday I would avoid crowds and queues as much as possible and if my husband drove to our side of the city I would try and walk to St John's at the other side of the city. My sister's words, 'they are not to be missed', just wouldn't go away.

My husband and I set out on the Tuesday morning. On arriving at the Redemptorist yard around 6.00 a.m., as I was going out the gate, a car had pulled up a little to my left and a man and woman were going in to the novena. Immediately I felt a strong urge or sensation — I cannot say what it was, but it was within me and had something to do with speaking to the couple. For some reason, I don't know why, I said, 'Ye are in early for the early session.' Instantly the woman looked at me and said, 'I know you. We went to school together in St Mary's.' I left school in 1954 — forty-seven years ago! We spoke for a few seconds and I said I was going to the relics. Her husband had gone in to the novena. She was leaving me, following him, and as she did so she turned and said, 'Do you want a drive to the relics?' I couldn't believe what I was hearing. There I was, with a leg that I didn't know would I be ever able to walk down, and if I got down would I be able to come back, and here I was getting a drive at 6.00 in the morning.

On the way down I said to her, 'You have no idea what this drive means to me. It must be St Thérèse.' She answered, 'It is St Thérèse. Fancy meeting you!'

On arrival in St John's she leant over as I was about to leave the car and kissed me on the cheek. She went her way. I went in to the relics and walked back to the car as if on air — no trace of a pain in my leg.

That morning my prayer and request to St Thérèse was to help me to talk to God better — the way my Carmelite sister, who can spend time in meditation and solitude, can — the way my sister in America, who gets up in the middle of the night and spends time every month in front of the Blessed Sacrament in adoration, can — the way my neighbour, who goes to prayer meetings and religious ceremonies, can. I could do none of those things — was trying to but just wasn't able. But, somehow, after coming home from the relics I felt a deep conviction within me: *No, don't be trying to do what they are doing, do it your own way.* And I had also, for the first time in my life, a huge awareness of God's love for us.

I am now totally at peace with my way of talking to God, and I know now God loves me as I am.

❦

FATHER DOMINIC JOHNSON, OSB, LIMERICK

We have a lovely stained-glass window in Glenstal Church, designed by the late Benedict Tutty OSB. The panel shows the two Teresas: Teresa of Ávila holding her quill, writing her journal; beneath her, Thérèse of Lisieux holding a cross. As a young monk, I went through a bad patch in my life (the dark night of the soul). Almost every night after Compline, I would pause before the panel and ask for help. Help came and the clouds lifted.

In homilies, I told the story of Thérèse doing the laundry with one of her sisters. The latter deliberately splashed the suds into Thérèse's eyes (no washing machines in those days). Thérèse just wiped the suds away and didn't retaliate. I know I would have

picked up the tub and poured it over my companion. I'm no saint
— I'm working on it!

❦

BERNIE POWER, DUBLIN

As a child I had often heard of St Thérèse the Little Flower. In my
parish church, a beautiful picture hung on a side altar; whenever I
passed it, I would say, 'St Thérèse, pray for us.' I had no great
devotion to her, as such. I suppose I just admired her more than
anything else.

In 1992, at a very low point in my life, I happened to go into a
church to pay a visit. There was a statue of St Thérèse in the corner.
I went over to it and I just stood there — looking, not praying. I must
have been there for about fifteen minutes. I didn't want to move,
and somehow, deep inside of me, I felt that she knew my pain.

A few days later, while driving to work, she came into my mind
and I found myself asking her to be my friend. I had many friends
whom I knew and loved, but somehow I felt that she could see
inside my soul. That week, I bought *Story of a Soul*.

It seemed to me that Thérèse's childhood was wonderful,
notwithstanding all of her emotional pain. It was all I would have
wished my own childhood to have been. Some time later I read
A Story of a Family and learned about her wonderful parents and
her lovely sisters. I began to understand how someone as holy
and as full of grace as Thérèse could live in a world full of sin.

As my relationship with Thérèse deepened, I began to see that
her love of God knew no bounds. Every breath, every sacrifice,
every act of love was for Him. I realised how short life's journey was

compared to an eternity with God. If I am annoyed with somebody and feel like hitting back, I can almost hear her saying: 'How would Jesus act?'

Today I converse with her more than pray to her, and I drink in her spirit, especially in the oratory at Hampton Hermitage. Frequently, that lovely image of her as an eight-year-old child standing beside her sister, Céline, comes to mind. It's as if she is there beside me, her little hand in mine, and there is a look on her face as if to say: 'Why are you so worried and upset?'

If I had the opportunity of speaking to Thérèse in eternity, I would tell her, face to face, how much her love of Jesus and her strength and her faith — even in her terrible darkness in the months leading up to her death — inspired me and strengthened me in my own darkness. During my lifetime, I have moved from being a person who had no real relationship with Thérèse to someone who has found in her a true and trusted friend.

🌹

ANNIE MASSEY, DUBLIN

Ever since I was a little girl I have had a great devotion to St Thérèse. I remember with my best friend and cousin, Peggy Timmons, God rest her, we used to go to St Joseph's Church, Glasthule, Sandycove, when we were teenagers, and kneel and pray before her beautiful statue, asking her to help us get the money to go to the pictures. I often went to St Joseph's also with my youngest sister, Agnes Barnes. She is now sixty-seven years old, married with five boys, and her health isn't the best; but she goes to Mass at seven o'clock every morning to that same church, and lights a candle for me and my family at the shrine of St Thérèse that we loved as children. Agnes is so good, and she often reminds me of those happy days when life was carefree, like a beautiful garden of flowers in summer.

After I was married to Frank, we had seven children, all girls. Following the birth of our two eldest daughters, Anna and Muriel, who were twins, we named our third daughter Teresa, after my favourite saint. I always encouraged them as children to pray to the Little Flower. And when we were struggling to make ends meet or get over a rough patch, I used to ask her to help us fix it up. She never let me down.

Dates associated with St Thérèse have happy and sad memories for me and my family. My mother-in-law, Catherine Massey, a lovely woman and a good friend, was born on 1 October, her feast day. Also, my husband Frank's birthday is on 3 October, what used to be her old feast day. However, the date that is burned into my heart and soul is 17 May, the anniversary of her canonisation. What should be a happy anniversary is one that broke my heart. On Friday, 17 May 1974, our eldest twin, Anna, was murdered in the Dublin and Monaghan bombings. She had just turned twenty-one the previous Sunday and was due to get married a few weeks later.

For several weeks I fought with God. My only consolation was a tiny framed photograph of St Thérèse as a three-year-old child which I had bought in a jumble sale and which I kept beside my bed. After Anna's horrific death I picked up the picture every night and cried, remembering Anna when she too was a beautiful child of that same age. I just asked St Thérèse to help me get through the pain and sorrow since I had six other daughters to take care of.

At a time when it would have been so easy to lose my faith in God, St Thérèse helped me to keep my faith. I ask St Thérèse every day to take care of Anna in Heaven until the day we are all reunited. That will be a very happy day, for, even though it is almost thirty years since we lost her, I still miss her greatly.

We put St Thérèse's picture on her gravestone, and I pray with her every day. I ask that God will forgive those who murdered Anna, and that our government, who abandoned us and lied to us, will one day honour Anna's memory, and the memory of all the other thirty-two murdered victims, by helping us with the truth. It's not too much to ask. Is it?

'... *the nature of love is to humble oneself....*'
Thérèse of Lisieux

Like a Member of Your Own Family

Interview with Jim Doyle
Co-driver of the Thérèsemobile

Don Mullan: What memorable moments do you have?

Jim Doyle: The most memorable point of the pilgrimage, as far as I am concerned, was the trip to the North of Ireland. I had never been North before, and I was absolutely amazed at the turnout — amazed at the friendliness of the people, in particular. We were always told down here, 'Oh, the Irish down here are very friendly and happy-go-lucky,' but I thought the people in the North had something more, something very special about them. My opinion of the North completely changed after the visit, although it only lasted nine days. It struck me that you could actually see what they had gone through over the last fifty or sixty years. You could see the pain in their eyes, and the suffering; and yet they were able to come out, be friendly.

DM: What was the story about the fish and chips?

JD: One of the few nights we had an hour to spare was down in Kinsale. We were fed up with the hotel food, so Pat said, 'Let's go out and we'll have sausage and chips.' We went into this restaurant; a little posh place, and the waitress came over. We picked up the menu and said, 'Sausage and chips for two, please.' She refused to serve us because it was only a kids' meal. So we left. We had to go out to a takeaway, and we sat down on a wall near the pier and ate fish and chips.

DM: Were there any other incidents?

JD: In Malahide people used to take photographs next to the Thérèsemobile. I saw this young girl, probably about twenty, standing beside the Thérèsemobile, and her mother was taking a photograph of her. I went over and put my arm around her and said to the mother, 'You might as well take one of me too.' She took the photograph. The mother came over to me and confided, 'You know, she only has six months to live.' There were sad moments like that.

DM: What was happening inside of you throughout the journey?

JD: It's very hard to explain. I had a feeling of great joy, as well as being emotional; we realised the importance of the job we were doing. Time was completely nonexistent. There were times we didn't even know what day it was; to check the dates we had to look at the programme. We never read a newspaper for the three months, we hadn't time.

DM: After your epic journey, how did you feel when you returned the relics to Lisieux?

JD: A few tears were shed. I felt emotionally drained and sad. I don't cry all that easy — no man does — but that day, I have to say, the tears came out of my eyes. 'Twas like leaving a sister behind, or a member of your own family. We got used to her, you know. It was very emotional, but I felt glad that everything went so well and we got her back safe.

'I attach no importance to dreams; besides, I have rarely had any meaningful dreams, even wondering why it is that I think of God all day long and yet am so little occupied with Him in my sleeping hours. I dream usually about such things as woods, flowers, streams, and the sea; I see beautiful children almost all the time; I catch butterflies and birds the like of which I've never seen before.'

Thérèse of Lisieux

'There are certain things that lose their perfume as soon as they are exposed to the air; there are deep spiritual thoughts which cannot be expressed in human language without losing their intimate and heavenly meaning....'
Thérèse of Lisieux

7

Beyond Rhyme and Reason

❦

M. BROGAN, MAYO

Mine is a very ordinary story. On the night that St Thérèse's relics lay in our cathedral, I brought two of my five children over to see her. They are aged sixteen and eighteen and came with me very readily. The sixteen-year-old boy was very taken aback at the many people there, especially the vast amount of teenagers. I had given him a short-stemmed rose in case he'd be embarrassed with a longer-stemmed one. I needn't have worried: he was amazed at the lads, his own age and older, proudly clutching their roses. Both he and his sister were deeply moved by our visit to the cathedral, and we left in a group, feeling we had been part of something special.

On arriving home at 12.30, I rang my twenty-two-year-old son and told him he should drop in to the church. I got a noncommittal answer and hung up. This lad is very much his own person, left school young and walks a little on the wild side and has caused me concern.

The next day my daughter and myself were in the church, having a last little chat with St Thérèse, when up the church marches my six-foot-two-inch twenty-two-year-old with his shaved head and two silver earrings in his ears. He touched St Thérèse's casket, made eye contact with me and left. At that moment I was prouder of him than if he had walked up to receive a law degree. I now felt St Thérèse had reached out to him and he to her. I asked her to look after my five kids and I know she will especially guide him. I also have the odd chat with her and feel she is very special.

🌹

KATHLEEN AND TRACEY BUCKLEY, CORK

Kathleen: Michaela is my one and only grand-daughter. She is three years old; at the time she was gone two and a half, she experienced a very dramatic time when a fire broke out in her bedroom where she played every morning. A very happy child she is.

We are indebted to two people that's very special in Michaela's life. One is Kieran Joyce, a good friend and I would say 'her guardian angel'. You see, Kieran, with great effort and persistence, endangered his own life to get Michaela out of the fire. There was an excessive amount of black smoke and thick toxic fumes coming from the room that was full of toys. I can't imagine the terror and fear that was in my grandchild.

Michaela was given a rose from a cousin, the night before — Catharine was her name — and that rose touched the relic of St Thérèse. The same night I went to a prayer meeting at a friend's house; she visited St Thérèse's relics that day, and she knew I had a fear of St Thérèse because of old wives' tales. You see, I always thought you bear a cross if you prayed to St Thérèse — call me old-fashioned if you want — but now I know different. She's our hero.

My friend gave me a piece of cloth that touched the relic and a beautiful prayer. I took them, as I didn't want to be rude, even though she knew how I felt. I carried on and read the prayer of St Thérèse that night. Somehow the words touched me in a special way. She said that she 'would bring you out of the darkness and into the light', and that's what she done for my grandchild Michaela.

Michaela was found after about twenty minutes — it's hard to say, with all the panic and fear and desperation — thanks to Kieran. He found her in my daughter Tracey's bedroom. He had a wet towel around his face; he crawled along the floors and could not see her. He felt her hand — he was led to her, I believe now, by St Thérèse. Michaela was brought out by Kieran, and Tracey was in shock. Tracey and Michaela were brought to the hospital for smoke inhalation, but it turned out that Michaela had no smoke in her lungs. She was covered from head to toe in black smoke, and also Kieran and Tracey. One could imagine the panic we went through. Still we get flashbacks of what could have happened to Michaela and Tracey.

The following day Kieran, Tracey and myself and Michaela's other grandmother and uncle went into the house and all the upstairs was gutted. We were lost for words, knowing what could have happened. Michaela's other grandmother Ann said to me, 'Kathleen, did you see the rose petals?' To our amazement, these rose petals, fresh as the day they were picked, were arranged in a semicircle. The leaves and the stem were at the opposite side of the petals. There was no way it was positioned by anyone in the house. It was fascinating, in the little corner alongside Tracey's bed. I picked up the petals and put them on my little grotto in my front room — I was given a present of a little statue of St Thérèse and again, I did not refuse it as it would be rude not to accept it. Now my family and I would be in debt to St Thérèse for the rest of our lives.

Being the little pet, Michaela keeps talking about the toys and her clothes — she loves her clothes. She lost everything in the fire. But the remarkable thing was that she had a doll that would say the 'Our Father' prayer. This was in the middle of all the burnt rubble of toys. The doll was still functional; it was a little smoked, but not burnt. It's hard to believe this, but it's a fact.

So when things got better Michaela and Tracey were at home with myself and the rest of the family; Michaela was talking about her lost things, and she was very stressed. I asked her what would I buy for her in town. She had a very tall order, but after she finished I said to her, 'What else do you want?' and she answered very quickly, 'I want a Holy God, Nanny.' And, as I have mentioned, I have a little grotto with a few statues in the front room and St Thérèse is one of them. So I asked her what Holy God did she want, so she went over to the grotto and said, 'That one, Nanny' — St Thérèse. And I said, 'Where did you see that before, baby?' She said, 'In the fire, in my Mammy's bedroom.' Of course this shocked us a great deal.

And not long after the fire, Michaela started saying things to Tracey about the fire: 'Mammy, the lady said, "In the name of the Father and of the Son and the Holy Spirit, amen,"' and made the sign of the cross while doing this. So Tracey asked her some questions and Michaela told Tracey that the lady told her to put a blanket over her head in the corner. Michaela was only over two-and-a-half at the time; how would a child that age say such things? So I know in my heart, and my family and friends know, St Thérèse spoke to her and blessed her in the fire.

The rose petals still are in my grotto, and now it's only fading but has a very strong scent coming from the petals still. Michaela goes out to the garden and picks petals and puts them on the grotto in the front room in front of St Thérèse. Sometimes she would cover the path with rose petals. Michaela never touched the roses in the garden before all of this. Little Michaela knew in her heart what went on.

Tracey: It was a usual Saturday morning, got out of bed to prepare my daughter Michaela's and my own breakfast, my next-door neighbour called in for a cup of tea. Just as I was putting down the two cups of tea on the table, I got a weird feeling over me as the kids were very quiet, so I ran up the stairs and was beaten back by very thick black smoke. I tried to get onto the landing to find the kids but I couldn't see or breathe. I found my way to the bathroom to open the window to try to leave in some light and leave the toxic fumes out, but it didn't work, the smoke was too much. I ran back downstairs for air.

I had the front door keyed and I was that panicky I couldn't think where the keys were, so Kieran Joyce (I owe my life to him also) climbed in the window and ran straight up the stairs. He was also beaten back down for air a couple of times. Daniel was got after about four or five minutes and there was still no sign of Michaela. Then Kieran wetted a bath towel for around his mouth and crawled along the floor to make his way into my bedroom; and there he found Michaela, huddled in the corner by my bed with a blanket over her head. It still puzzles me, the cleverness of Michaela to come out of the room of the fire (her room) and go into my bedroom.

So anyway, Kieran brought her down in his arms and she was silent and I thought she was gone and I was screaming, but she was in shock. I couldn't leave go of her. They took us away in an ambulance and I hyperventilated, and all I kept saying was, 'I couldn't even save my own child.' That thought needled my head for weeks. Kieran Joyce wasn't even supposed to be there, as he was supposed to be training in the boxing club that day, so it was fate he was there.

The next day my mother and Michaela's other Nan went into the house and into my room to look where Michaela was hiding, and they noticed the rose petals in a semicircle in front of the corner where Michaela was hiding. They were fresh; this was remarkable, because even the shampoo bottles and toiletries in the bathroom were melted to a crisp by the heat. So Mam said this to Kieran, and he also said he noticed the semicircle of petals around Michaela when he found her in the room. So we brought the rose petals into my mam's house and put them on her little grotto in the front room.

Since the fire Michaela's doing all unusual actions — for example, picking rose petals out in my mam's garden whenever she's up there, going around blessing anyone who comes in, and talking about the little statue of St Thérèse and telling St Thérèse she loves her and she's her lady. Also, Michaela and myself started talking in bed one night about it, and she told me that during the fire there was a lady in her room talking. Michaela said that the lady said, 'In the name of the Father and the Son and the Holy Spirit, amen,' and Michaela said this quite plain, like an adult, and made the sign of the cross while saying this. So I started crying again, and in my eyes my little girl is very special.

How we came about to know that it was St Thérèse was the Monday after the fire, we were going into town to buy new clothes for Michaela and my mam asked Michaela what she wanted in town. So she said, 'New clothes, teddy bears and sweets,' and my mam said, 'Do you want anything else, Michaela?' And she replied, 'I want Holy God.' So we looked at her and asked what Holy God did she want and would she show us; so she pointed over to Mam's grotto, which had a lot of holy statues, and she pointed out St Thérèse. We asked her where did she see her before, and

Michaela replied, 'In Mammy's bedroom, in the fire; she talked to me.' So I don't doubt those instances are true, as how could a young child come out with such remarks? To this day, a couple months after the fire, Michaela is fascinated with statues, so I think I have a little nun on my hands. I also owe my life and respect to St Thérèse for taking a great part in saving my child's life.

CHRIS MAVERLEY, LEADING FIRE OFFICER, CORK FIRE BRIGADE

Cork Fire Brigade received a 999 call at 11.51 a.m. on 23 June 2001. We arrived at 9c Glengarriff Road, Fairhill, Cork, at 11.57 a.m.

A fire was concentrated in bedrooms upstairs. The room from which Michaela Buckley was rescued was full of dense smoke and heat. It is my opinion that the child was in imminent danger, particularly from toxic fumes. But for the prompt action of Kieran Joyce, who rescued Michaela shortly before we arrived, the consequences could have been tragic.

Our estimate of damage caused to the house by the fire was £20,000.

❧

DAIRE WHELAN, DUBLIN

Grotesque, macabre, horrifying, even sickening. When I heard about the visit of St Thérèse and her bones, and read the hype about the imminent 'tour', I couldn't believe what I was hearing. Why would anyone in their right mind go see a dead nun's bones from the nineteenth century? Surely as a country we had moved on from this glorification of Catholicism. Had we not moved out from the community built upon publicans and parish priests to the wider European notion of inclusion and eclecticism? Were we to see a return to the embarrassing images of the Nuncio's visit in the 1930s or the Pope in the late 1970s — a time when reverence was accordingly given and our humble places noted?

But, despite my protestations, the curiosity still got the better of me. The relics of St Thérèse were visiting my hometown of Malahide, and the nuns, priests, shopkeepers, Gardaí were out in force to make it a welcome of sorts. At the prompting of my mother, we both decided to have a look. Now, we're not a religious family; Christ, I can't remember the last time I was at church — though I'm sure He could tell me. But, well, the power of advertising does work. 'She's bigger than Madonna'; 'She's one of the real All Saints', the posters told us. And I just had to find out. At least to prove me wrong — or justify my ever-growing cynicism.

Walking up the hill under the stars, joining the throngs of elderly (and young) to queue into the church, was not my road to Damascus; but, for the first time in a long time, there was a sense of community — of going out of good spirit, and doing it with many like-minded people.

Entering the church, the sounds of 'Ave Maria' first struck me and reminded me that now was the time to don the picture of piety. And there she was in all her entirety — well, what was left in the casket, anyway — commanding centre stage, with the ornate wooden casket in a protective glass case. People were touching it, praying to it; some were even weeping, overcome by it all. Me? I was just thinking how many bones you could fit in that space, and why did it have to be in a glass case?

For it wasn't the presence of the relics that struck me, but the pervading atmosphere of serenity. Yes, I know: cue Gregorian chant and monks in white robes. But the little church was packed to the rafters and there was a constant stream of in-flowing people. But we all just sat there, in complete silence, letting the music and presence create the atmosphere. For the first time since probably my granddad's funeral fifteen years ago, I didn't feel awkward, didn't feel out of place, didn't not want to be there.

I sat there with my thoughts and just pondered. My mind drifted to places away from pending exams, relationship problems and money. And the brimming church at midnight that night was, I'm sure, the same. It wasn't really about the bones or the legacy. For me it became a small moment that brought me back into the fold of the Church and community — something the formalised, inhibiting practice of Mass misses.

The truth was, this was something different, an occasion — a touring event that seems to have aroused the curiosity of thousands and awakened a deeper sense of spirit. I've no desire to return to Mass and confess a lifetime of sins; but, for once, I felt a belonging in my religion and saw a glimpse of what faith could mean. Maybe, just maybe, it's what our city needed to shake it from its spiralling stupor. But, sure, I'm only a cynic, so why should I care?

❦

SISTER NOREEN KEANE, RSM, LIMERICK

I was sitting on a chair near the reliquary at the top of St John's Cathedral, watching the crowds pass by and trying to pray. A group of young travelling people came in and stood near me. One little fellow of about seven or eight asked me what was in the 'box'. I told him it contained the bones of a very holy young nun called Thérèse. His next question: 'Why don't they open it and let us see them?' So, to mitigate his disappointment at not being able to see into the 'box', I began to tell him something about the saint — her family, her parents, etc., and how she loved God very, very much.

His next question caught me unawares: 'Are you her cousin?' Hastening to disillusion him on that score, I could not but be struck at the implication of his question. Because I seemed to know so much about Thérèse, he concluded I must be related to her! His own culture was coming out.

I was touched, and hopefully more humble, after that encounter with one of God's 'little ones'.

❦

MARY D. O'CONNOR, CORK

I am a young entrepreneur of the age of twenty-nine. While not a very devout Catholic, I do, however, pray a lot — not really novenas or anything like that, but I talk to both St Thérèse and St Bernadette. My love for both came from when I was young (circa fourteen years, when my grandmother, whom I was very close to, died); I read books on both and followed on from there. As a general rule, almost every night (apart from the odd night I came home after a night on the town) since the age of fourteen, on going to bed I would say, 'Good night, God; good night, Nannie (my grandmother); St Thérèse, I love you.' It wasn't that I felt particularly drawn to her or anything; it was just something I did.

About seven years ago I worked for the Southern Health Board in Tralee. While there I befriended an elderly workmate who told me of a novena to St Thérèse, where you say the 'Glory be to the Father' to her so many times a day for so many weeks — I can't for the life of me remember the exact amount now. My workmate continued telling me, 'If you keep this novena, you will get the sign of the rose.' So I began to say the 'Glory be to the Father' any time I would think about it. I just got into the habit of saying it over and over every time I went for walks, etc.; I still do to this day.

I had a rose hanging on my wall, a replica from the Rose of Tralee Festival — you know, one of those roses that blinks light, worked on a battery. Anyway, it was on my wall for at least a year or two, and to my knowledge the battery would have been long dead, as it hadn't blinked for years. One night — in the middle of the night, in fact — during the time I was saying this novena, the rose fell from the wall and started to blink. It had never happened before. I am a sound sleeper, and the sound of it had woken me up. I nearly died of fright, to put it mildly. I had my sign. My faith in St Thérèse really began from there.

Anyway, moving on, I heard she was coming to Ireland. Now, may I reiterate that I am not a devout person; I never go to Mass, unless when I visit home; I am a typical young person who drinks, smokes the odd time, etc., so I wouldn't be entirely religious. In fact, when one hears me talking, my bad language can often be very offensive; it's just a habit I have. So when I tell people that I do pray, they find it very hard to believe.

I visited St Thérèse in Cork, at the North Cathedral. I persuaded my two friends to come along with me. We were queuing all the way in and were having a good laugh, talking about people, the usual chitchat. When we entered the cathedral, everyone was praying, but again I did not feel particularly devout. We joined in our prayers and were up to the relic before we knew it. I must admit I did feel a little disappointed when I saw the small size of the relic, and didn't feel in any way excited or anything.

When I touched the relic I said the 'Glory be to the Father' in my mind. As I left the relic and lifted my hand, I felt light-headed all of a sudden. It is very hard to describe. I knew I wouldn't faint; I've felt like fainting before, but it wasn't like that. It was more like describing being drunk and feeling that you're swaying from side to side; my head was spinning. I found a seat nearby and sat down. We stayed for a while, but I still felt my head swaying and felt very weak. May I reiterate that I had not drunk that night, as I had gone to dancing classes, and am in perfect health, not at all weak? In fact, the cathedral wasn't even hot, and I had my jacket off, so it wasn't from heat or anything.

When we got home I still felt absolutely weak. The girls, one of whom lived with me for four years, had never seen me like this; they said I was as white as a ghost and didn't at all look well. Again, I will say I am always healthy, never sick. The girls stayed up with me for another while until I felt better; I didn't get any stronger and in the end went to bed. I was fine the next morning, but couldn't help feeling that St Thérèse somehow reached out to me there in that cathedral.

Now, I don't know if it was the excitement or the atmosphere, that I became emotional, or what. I don't think so because, as I was saying earlier, we had been talking of different things so I hadn't built it up in my mind. I have no explanation as to why I suddenly felt so weak and my head was spinning; it has never happened to me before or since. All that I can say is that I felt as if St Thérèse was somehow reaching out to me. Could that be so?

❧

PHIL KEHOE, WEXFORD

In 1967 I took my mother on a three-month tour of Europe, visiting all the well-known shrines. We started with a visit to Fatima, then moved on to Lisbon. After that we spent a week in Lourdes, and when we got to Paris my mother requested to visit Lisieux, the home of St Thérèse. At this stage, my finances were being severely stretched, so I was unable to grant her request. My mother was most disappointed, and I wondered about this saint who seemed to have such an impact on her.

Thirty-four years passed, and on Easter Sunday, 15 April 2001, St Thérèse's relics passed within a few hundred yards of my house, en route to Enniscorthy. I feel that St Thérèse did me the honour of visiting me when I wasn't in a position to visit her! Or perhaps my deceased mother finally got her wish to introduce me to St Thérèse of Lisieux?

❧

MARTINA AUGHNEY, CARLOW

[My husband] John and I had decided to go down to Rosslare that Easter weekend and take our son Sean for a small break. I was seven months pregnant, and John had everything arranged. When we got there, we were told that the relics were expected in the harbour around 10.30 and going to St Patrick's Church from there. The woman advised us that if we wanted to get a good view of the ship carrying Thérèse, we could go down to the banks behind Hotel Rosslare. So we did.

When we got there, the sense of excitement and anticipation began to grow in me, and I began to get impatient, scanning the sea for her ship. One woman told us that the ferry wasn't due in owing to bad weather from France for at least another hour, but I knew it wouldn't take that long to get here. About fifteen minutes later, I saw a ship; don't ask me how I knew she was on this ship, but I did. I was almost in tears as the ferry drew nearer. I kept telling John, 'She's on it, she's here.'

As I kept my eyes glued to the ferry, I saw Thérèse right over the ship. She was dressed in her habit, a black or brown veil, a cream-coloured cape clasped at the front, and just a glimpse of her dress or tunic underneath. She had her arms outstretched over the ship and she was looking directly down on it.

I thought I was seeing things, and I blinked, but as the *Normandy* came closer to the harbour I saw her again — same position, but this time she was looking up to the bank and a lot closer to me. [It] seemed she was smiling, and her face was radiant. It was as if she wanted everyone to come down to meet her, and the deep joy in my heart must have showed on my face. How I longed to run down the pathway to the harbour, but of course I couldn't, as I was seven months pregnant.

When we got in finally to St Patrick's and made our way up to her casket, I kept asking her to bless my unborn child and pleading with her to let the child be born healthy, as Sean was born with a narrow main artery in his heart, a tiny hole and a duct that didn't close up after birth — he's fine now, after being operated on. I waited for John, who had Sean asleep in his arms; he approached the reliquary, put his hand on it, eyes closed, and began to break down. He spent at least fifteen minutes just standing there in the same position, oblivious to the people around him.

We saw her again in Carlow two days later. I kissed the casket, put my hand on it. I didn't want to leave her. John knew I didn't want to leave, so he got me a seat on the altar. It was like chatting and being with an old friend. She was in front of me and I just kept looking at her, smiling and yet wishing she was beside me, alive, and us talking away like two best friends.

On Saturday, while driving down to Kilkenny, I just closed my eyes for a while and I could see her, in front of the cross. She had just got her picture taken by Céline and we were walking around the courtyard in the Carmel in Lisieux when she saw us. I had the baby in my arms; John had Sean by the hand. I could see her face. When she saw me and the baby she ran up to me, skirts flying, and breathless. She couldn't believe I'd had the baby. She wanted to hug me so I asked John would he mind holding Michael. Thérèse gave me a big hug, she held Michael (we had been told I was expecting a boy) and Sean was tugging at her cloak. I took Michael. She lifted Sean up and threw him in the air; he was laughing, she was laughing, clearly delighted. I woke up then, smiling. That was the beginning.

One week later we [went to Gort Muire]. We didn't know how to get there; John bought a map, and I kept asking her, 'Thérèse, show us where to go, lead us to you' — and she did! When I saw her it was as if she was waiting for us. I cried, and Sean touched the relic and he was glued to it, a little soul gazing in wonderment at what was before him. Now every time he sees her picture he gets excited, points to her, and even when he sees any nun, he thinks it Thérèse.

A few weeks later, the May Bank Holiday, we decided yet again to go on another small break, as I had only a month to go. We chanced Greystones, as it's near Dublin, in case the baby decided he wanted out. Before we left we had the TV on, morning Mass from Knocklyon, and I saw Thérèse's casket on the altar. John sat down on the couch — he wasn't in the best of form, he was beginning to doubt her friendship, while I could feel her around me. I asked her to reassure him. When he saw her on the altar and heard her message from the priest he broke down. I told him she was trying to get through to him, to trust her.

Again, that week I was still having dreams of her, and the next Sunday, 13 May, I just said to John, 'Why don't we go to St Joseph's Church?' I felt her urging us to go. So we did, but I wanted to spend more time than we could with her, what with the crowds there. As my blood pressure was giving me trouble, we left. We had planned to go to Whitefriar Street after my antenatal check-up a few days later, but I was admitted to hospital, so John went instead.

Later on that week, while I was in hospital, I talked to this girl who had trouble (i.e. drugs). She spoke of her worries and fears. I got my bag, spoke to her of Thérèse, gave her a prayer card and the itinerary, blessed her with the beads, and she then kept saying the prayer and kissing the picture. Another girl who was barely twenty was overdue, so I gave her the beads. She blessed herself, kissed the medal, and five minutes later was induced and went into labour. I felt Thérèse was working through me to help those two young women. Please God, that first girl has got her life together, off drugs and making a new life for herself and her daughter and baby.

When I got out of hospital, that Sunday, I felt an urge yet again to see Thérèse, this time in Drogheda. I said it to John — he thought I was cracked. We went just the same, and we thought it'd be our last time to spend time with her. I was overjoyed to see her but fearful for her because I knew she'd be going from Drogheda to the North. I felt that some hard-line Unionists would react badly to her visit. So when I walked up to her I kissed the relic, laid my hand on it for what seemed a long time, and told her to be careful, as I'd say to anyone who meant a lot to me. When we went to sit down, John broke down yet again, at the thought of never seeing her again. Now, I don't know how or why, but as I was sitting right beside a statue of her I knew we'd see her again.

A few days later, I was admitted back into the Coombe for blood-pressure monitoring, and I was feeling a bit low, so I turned on the TV and saw a report of Thérèse's visit. She was with me. That same night I saw a report on her relics crossing the Border. So that helped me a lot. I was up North in '93. I fell in love with the countryside and I thought Belfast is a beautiful yet badly wounded city. I pray that Thérèse's visit has given a little bit of hope to people who have lost all hope of deliverance from their terrible cross.

A few weeks later, I was in for my last antenatal check-up. My baby boy was due the following week, only I was told he would be overdue, perhaps up to a week or ten days. Thérèse was leaving that Thursday — or so we thought — and I suddenly said, 'She's playing tricks on us; she wants us to go to Tallow! Now that the baby's overdue, she wants us to come down.' John just shook his head, said 'The little monkey woman,' and the two of us laughed.

That weekend we went down. John saw a report on the visit, showed it to me and I was over the moon to discover she was staying on for a further four to five days. So she'd be with me when I gave birth that coming Wednesday.

We got there; the crowds were knee-deep in places. I got a blessing and when the time came to venerate, it was like the

January sales: people wouldn't make space for a woman about to give birth within a few days. But John knew how much I longed to see her again and made sure I got up to her. I was so tired and exhausted and it must have showed, because when I finally got up to her I almost fainted. I just managed to touch her casket and was about to speak to her in my heart — I never got the chance, as people had to pull me away from her. I kept saying I'd be OK, but of course I wasn't; I had to sit down.

It was as if she knew I wasn't all right. I didn't feel her urging me to visit her again, but I constantly felt her with me, as I did while in hospital. Deep down I knew I wasn't alone. My adopted little sister was with me. Even when I finally gave birth, after being three days overdue, I recovered very quickly. And my second child, Michael, was eight and a half pounds, a fine healthy baby.

When she left these shores and I saw her departure on television, I cried as if my heart would break. She had come to mean so much to me. I believed she had left us altogether, but I was wrong. As it happens, I'm due to go to St Vincent's Hospital shortly to get a ganglion or cyst on my right hand removed. Last Friday, while feeding Michael, I felt an icy chill along my left side, in front of my knees and right hand. I just said to John, 'She's here.' And while going into Carlow later on I felt pain, and was about to say to John, 'I can't wait to get this lump off', when I looked at the back of my hand where the cyst was, and I thought I was seeing things: it had gone completely. I was so happy. I knew who was behind it. It was my loving friend Thérèse.

God knows how I'm going to explain this to my doctor.

❦

JIM AND DEBORAH, SAN DIEGO

Jim: I live in San Diego, Southern California. I am the youngest of a large family from Belfast and can remember how Mum (God rest her) would donate pennies (few and far between for us) to the Sisters of the Little Flower.

I was very fortunate to visit the Golden Cathedral containing Thérèse's remains when it passed through San Diego. The chapel at the Catholic University was full to capacity, and my girlfriend Deborah and I had to stand in the aisles.

Although Deborah had never met my mum, she had seen the one photograph of her which I have carried with me since I left home twenty years ago. As Deborah and I waited and the congregation rotated to receive Communion, I saw Mum ahead of us, waiting in line. She turned and looked straight at me and smiled.

Needless to say, I was astounded and, heart racing, I tried to get up behind her. I was torn between elation and anguish, as I lost her as quickly as she had appeared....

When Mass let out, devotions said, Deborah and I left. On the drive home, Deborah, without looking at me, just asked, 'Did you see your mum? I noticed she was wearing that dress you got her.' Deborah actually mentioned it to me first.

The feelings evoked at the time of the incident were real. I've pondered this many times and know that, of all the saints, considering Mum's devotion, Thérèse would have been the most likely catalyst to let me know Mum was in good hands.

Deborah: We were at the viewing of St Thérèse's remains on Christmas Eve morning. There was standing room only, so we were in an apse. I tend to be an observer when I'm in a crowd, and so I was looking around at all the different people when I noticed a diminutive, elderly lady who looked just like the photo of Jim's mom, the only photo of her I've seen. The same floral print dress, the same way her jaw was set. I watched her take Communion and then waited for her to come out the other end of the Communion line, because I wanted to get over to her and get a closer look at her.

Even though I watched her intently, I didn't see her come out the other end of the line. I immediately started watching both exits, but never caught sight of her again. I looked for her all during the rest of the service and again outside. I had my eyes peeled for her, but she was gone.

❧

CARMEL CUNNINGHAM, DONEGAL

Believe it or not, it was Bertie Ahern — or, rather, a missed opportunity to shake hands with the great man — that persuaded me to throw all my ifs, ands and buts to the wind and queue up to touch the glass case containing the casket in which the relics of St Thérèse lay. And this is how it all began....

[When I first heard that the relics of St Thérèse would be travelling around Ireland,] I could not believe it! They were at it again — shooting themselves in the foot. One more pyro-technic display of medieval mind-set in the twenty-first century. They were going to hawk St Thérèse's relics up and down the country like some curio in a travelling medicine show! The idea of the bones on parade was utterly repugnant to me; I knew I would not go near the relics, as the whole procedure smacked of shamanism.

Around this time, I had decided to attend the WOW [Women's Ordination Worldwide] conference in UCD at the end of June. Soline Vatinel sent me a piece she had written on St Thérèse, who, like Soline, had wished to be ordained a priest. Even with my new insights into her thoughts on women's ordination, I still felt that going to see the 'bones' sniffed of something pre-Luther, something Chaucer would have sniggered at!

Anyway, the day arrived. That same day my husband, a colleague of his and I were actually leaving Letterkenny to see another miraculous presence — Bertie Ahern was visiting Gweedore and we had been invited to meet him. Despite having virtually no interest in political parties, as opposed to politics — yes, work that one out! — I was looking forward to seeing our 'leader' in the flesh. Then the thought struck me: I must go to see St Thérèse the same way I went to see Bertie. It didn't mean that I had the mind of a medieval Catholic if I did go, just as it didn't mean I had to be a card-carrying member of Fianna Fáil if I shook hands with Mr Ahern. (Actually, that didn't happen; I didn't crush forward soon enough, and I missed my opportunity of pressing the flesh with An Taoiseach. Drat!) I also thought that I should have taken one of my kids, who is interested in politics, with me to see Bertie — and then another thought struck. My kids could possibly meet Bertie some other time, some other place, but when would St Thérèse be back in Letterkenny? I could not wait to get my husband bundled into the car and home.

As soon as we arrived at the house, I corralled my three children into the Honda — it was about 10.30 p.m. — and headed for the cathedral. It was raining, so, having seen the number of cars and the crowd of people, we decided to get chips and go home. My younger daughter went next door to a sleepover. My son went to bed and Eleanor, my sixteen-year-old, and I sat watching TV.

Some time after 1.00 a.m., the 'compulsion' struck again. We would try again to touch the glass case containing the casket. We dug my son out of bed. We, three of us, headed for the cathedral. Still crowds. Still raining. I looked at the kids; enthusiasm was not written on their faces. We returned home.

Dawn. My husband had left early in the morning to go to a football match. Just before 9.30 a.m., the psycho-magnetic-traction-beams emanating from the casket jolted me out of bed. *We'll do it this time!*

To my amazement, the queues had gone. Mass had just started. My son loves Mass/saints/praying, so he was in his element; my daughter was glad she had gone; and I, having let gut feelings ride over taste and logic, was actually feeling very happy and peaceful that I had decided to witness this unique event. I felt good that I had come to pay homage to a grand wee girl who just happened to be one of the greatest saints of the Catholic Church. That shy look, that enigmatic smile, belied an unbending will. This Little Flower was no shrinking violet! Even some of the pieces she had written — for example, her concept of prayer — were gentle on the surface but ironic underneath. Then it started to dawn on me why I liked her. She was a woman full of contradictions.

Could it be that Thérèse was a 'rebel with a cause', incognito, deep in the power structure of the Church? This Doctor of the Church, a woman, believed in the ordination of other women. The 'coincidental' arrival of her relics in Ireland drew attention to the first ever WOW Conference. At the same time, the Vatican — i.e., men! — was 'dissuading' other great women such as Sr Joan

Chittister and Sr Myra Poole from attending. I began to feel that if the traditionalists in the Church thought they had left Catholicism in safe hands, Thérèse's hands, they were in for a rude awakening.

Thérèse may be the catalyst for change, as people, nation by nation, begin to reflect on their responses to her relics' visit and consider the meaning of Christianity and what, if anything, various 'traditions' have to do with it. For, at best, traditions are to truth and life what painting by numbers is to the Renaissance or a merry-go-round ride is to saddling up for the Grand National! At worst, the handiwork of tradition is *bloody* evident among such religious peoples as those who inhabit Northern Ireland or the Middle East, because it gives gross unthinking ignorance a cosy bed in which to spawn and rote-like stagnation a place in which to fester. Remember, it was not the safe, traditional son who got the fatted calf! Great saints — and Thérèse is one of them — were never bound by tradition. They realised that traditions are man-made, not God-given, and can — and should — be broken any time they endanger body or soul or both!

Anyway, back to the cathedral, where Mass had ended. We started to queue. It was wonderful to see so many people enjoying being in church. People were happy. People were talking. There was an air of excitement, of anticipation tinged with awe — what you'd expect when the divine touches the mortal. Absolutely no disrespect. Just people delighted to be there. Just people sensing otherworldliness. Just people being human. For one brief moment I felt, 'Yes! Mother Church, take me back — I'm all yours. You have changed, and you have changed me.'

Then reality struck. Someone shushed us to be quiet. He decided to share with us his illusion that silence was synonymous with respect. And I, piqued, thought, 'God forbid that a person should feel joyful or emotional or spiritual at a Catholic service. That would certainly fly in the face of tradition.' But as those words careered headlong to my lips, they were stopped abruptly by the red light of reason, and I realised I was doing it myself now — the old religious intolerance bit. If we were all supposed to be the same, God would not have created us different. So I looked up, doe-eyed, into the shusher's countenance, and beamed him my most charismatic smile.

When I lowered my eyes again, I found myself in front of the casket. I ran my fingers over the glass. 'If Jesus is all things to all people,' I thought, 'then you, Thérèse, are His most perfect emulator, His most perfect ambassador.' She had come to people who, for a whole variety of reasons, would probably never have gone to her. Her mission impossible to Letterkenny was now a *fait accompli*.

Shortly afterwards, I bade farewell to the relics of St Thérèse of Lisieux. Would this be 'Goodbye till we meet again, Little Flower'? Or perhaps it was 'Adieu — goodbye forever.' Which would it be, Thérèse? (I still don't know.) You have touched my life, but as yet I'm not sure how. *Merci beaucoup*.

'… a little bit of bitterness is at times preferable to sugar.'

Thérèse of Lisieux

'When the human heart gives itself to God, it loses nothing of its innate tenderness; in fact, this tenderness grows when it becomes more pure and more divine.'
Thérèse of Lisieux

8

Dissenting Views

❧

ANONYMOUS, ULSTER

You propose to write a book concerning the decadent bones of a young, single sinner female whose soul may be in hell, as she was a devoted Roman Catholic. That system is anti-Bible and has no support in the Word of God. The position of Scripture regarding Peter as first pope is entirely wrong. Jesus is the rock and upon him — not Peter — the Church is built. Research your RC teaching and don't be one of the blind leading the blind. Souls are saved by Jesus and the Word of God. It has absolutely nothing to do with baptism, Sacraments, holy water, Mass, penance, rosary beads, the priesthood, vigils, candles, processions, Confessions, pilgrimages and the whole totally misleading and confusing assortment of the baggage that constitutes Roman Catholicism. Pray tell me, do you know if your soul is right with God? Is it saved? If not, you die as a good Roman Catholic to awaken to the reality that purgatory is nonexistent and judgement and hell is staring you in the face. How much will allegiance to the Pope and all he represents help you on that vital eternal moment when you die?

Morbid? Offensive? No! I am concerned about your eternal soul and destination. God has provided salvation in Christ. God did not institute the Roman faith — that is a system totally foreign to the Word of God. The Word of God exalts the Son of God. Rome exalts its adherents. Think of the pride and exaltation of Rome's cardinals, bishops, saints and religious orders, fraternities, convents, right down to the exaltation of the priests in the chapels. Christ is the one who should be exalted.

Think this through, as your soul is at stake. Die an RC, or repent and get to Heaven the Bible way. The choice is personal. Flee to Christ — your saviour. Forsake a system that enslaves you as a sinner to its claims and teachings, which you or any other RC can never attain unto. Work and keep and do all that Rome/priest/pope teaches, and still die a sinner. What an awful thought — but true! Choose you: Rome or the Word of God. Eternity beckons, one breath away. Christ came into the world to save sinners. You are a sinner (Rom. 3:23).

❦

JAMES K. GARDINER, DERRY

Being a Christian in the reformed tradition, I know little about this saint. There is one thing, however, I am sure of, and that is: 'It is better to trust in the Lord than to put confidence in princes' (Psalms 118 and 9). 'God is spirit and they that worship him must worship him in spirit and in truth' (St John 4:24).

It seems to me that the saint's remains should be reverently buried and left to rest in peace until Resurrection Day, when all shall stand before God and give an account. Until then, our faith must be directed to someone living.

'Have faith in God' (St Mark 11:22).

❦

ANONYMOUS, DUBLIN

I suggest you write a book on the brave women of Ireland, who, while they were in the slums and could neither feed nor clothe their children, were ordered to have one baby a year under pain of going to a mythical place called 'Hell'. The Church promoted itself by promoting signs, wonders, apparitions — and a brilliant Jesuit who left the Church said so. Do write a book on their descendants, who are today sleeping in streets, committing suicide, dying of drugs. The Church was comfortable with their sad, hungry lives, while they ate and drank well.

What did Thérèse ever do to help the world? She prayed and died young. What an achievement! Her bones were carted around Ireland, which was pure superstition, and the gullible people love it. They never think for themselves. It's a case of 'Father said, so it must be right and we must oblige.'

Thank God today's youth are better educated and moving statues will only amuse them. If you have time to spare, do go and help the homeless and stop promoting the superstition. It worked well for the Church, which is the best-oiled public relations company in the world and the wealthiest and still looks for our donations.

'Poor women, how they are misunderstood! And yet they love God in much larger numbers than men do and during the Passion of Our Lord, women had more courage than the apostles since they braved the insults of the soldiers and dared to dry the adorable Face of Jesus.'
Thérèse of Lisieux

9

Reflections

SOLINE VATINEL, DUBLIN

Earlier this year, Ireland was host both to the relics of St Thérèse of Lisieux and to the first international conference on the ordination of women in the Catholic Church (organised by WOW — Women's Ordination Worldwide). The two events were organised independently, and initially the relics were to leave Ireland on 28 June, eve of the conference; however, a change of plan resulted in the two events actually overlapping. Coincidence or Providence?

The answer to this question depends, of course, on one's standpoint. Some, at first glance, will have seen the visit of the relics and the conference as being poles apart, expressing the particular agendas of, respectively, the 'conservative' and 'liberal' wings of the Church. However, as one who had the joy and the privilege of participating in both events (along with many others), I see it in a very different light. I believe that it was very right and fitting that the relics of St Thérèse were in Ireland while the WOW conference was taking place. Why? Because of St Thérèse's deep sense of vocation to the priesthood, which has led to her adoption as 'patron saint' by many of the groups praying and working for the ordination of women in the Catholic Church. So it was just like Thérèse to arrange to be in Ireland for the conference!

A small group of us from BASIC (Brothers and Sisters in Christ) went down to Rosslare Harbour very early on Easter Sunday, to greet the arrival of the relics. We carried placards with the words 'WELCOME, SAINT THÉRÈSE, CALLED TO BE A PRIEST'. To our great surprise and delight, we featured that evening on RTÉ television news, together with a brief interview with Bishop Brendan Comiskey confirming that her vocation to the priesthood is well documented. This surely must register as one of Thérèse's first miracles on her Irish visit — to broadcast to the whole nation her desire to be a priest. For, while it is indeed well documented, it had also been kept well hidden ... that is, until St Thérèse set foot in Ireland and proclaimed it from the rooftops!

When the relics passed by me that bright Easter morning, I was filled with a deep sense of joy. I felt the continuity between her and women like myself: the same deep desire to be a priest, in a Church which opens itself painfully slowly to the reality of the fullness of God in women. I felt, as never before, her affirmation and encouragement in our efforts to make known publicly what she had discovered in the silence of her Carmelite cell over a hundred years ago: the good news that God calls women, as well as [men], to the ordained. I certainly experienced some of the vitality of the Resurrection that morning in Rosslare!

As we were in the throes of preparing to host the WOW conference and labouring under severe official disapproval, we were very glad of the support Thérèse could lend us through her intercession. We were not disappointed! When our keynote speaker was forced to withdraw under pressure at the eleventh hour, we received one of

Thérèse's promised roses as a replacement: *Rose* Hudson-Wilkin, a priest in the Church of England (which, incidentally, shows that Thérèse, like God, is truly ecumenical!) The WOW conference was immensely blessed in a thousand ways — not least in the way that the threatened sanctions against some of the speakers and organisers vanished like snow in sunshine. I was glad to have the opportunity to go and say a heartfelt 'Thank you' to Thérèse of Lisieux.

Thérèse promised that she would spend her Heaven doing good on Earth. One of the ways she is fulfilling her promise is by helping so many of us women both to welcome wholeheartedly our calling to priesthood as coming from God, and to remain faithful to the Church which until now denies it. It is because Thérèse herself was intimately acquainted with this state of prophetic tension, and because she lived it with the utmost creativity that is the fruit of love, that she is able to guide us in this daring journey.

At this stage, it may be necessary for me to stress that I am neither reducing Thérèse to her calling to the priesthood, nor even suggesting for a moment that it is the most important dimension of her life. Love is the defining meaning of her life, and she breathed her last confirming it: 'My God ... I love you.' If I have such a deep respect and affection for Thérèse — she is for me like a beloved sister — it is because she surrendered every fibre of her being to Love. Her abiding desire to be a priest is only one expression of this, and Thérèse never experienced her desire to be a priest as being in conflict with her desire to be a saint. In this respect, she was no different from countless men for whom the desire for ordination has not been an impediment to subsequent canonisation!

Official Church statements on Thérèse have been very careful not to breathe a word on this dangerous topic. After all, for a good

Catholic girl to entertain the desire to be a priest is tantamount to having a bad thought. So Thérèse, this model of Christian humility and obedience, this Doctor of the Church, couldn't have done what only faithless, misguided radical feminists are meant to do!

However, the records show us quite clearly that Thérèse believed she had an authentic calling to the priesthood, that she often spoke about it and that it preoccupied her until the end of her life. In fact, it is truly remarkable that it is this vocation to priesthood which provides her with meaning and consolation when facing her early death. This is expressed very plainly and very movingly in the testimony that her sister Céline, her closest confidante (Sr Geneviève in religion), gave under oath at the Beatification process in 1910:

> In 1897, but before she was really ill, Sister Thérèse told me that she expected to die that year. Here is the reason she gave me for this in June. When she realised that she had pulmonary tuberculosis, she said: 'You see, God is going to take me at an age when I could not have had time to become a priest.... If I could have been a priest, I would have been ordained at these June ordinations. So, what did God do? So that I would not be disappointed he let me be sick: in that way I couldn't have been there, and I would die before I could exercise my ministry.'*

And Céline adds, 'The sacrifice of not being able to be a priest was something she always felt very deeply.'

Céline's testimony continues with an extraordinary revelation, which indicates how much Thérèse believed in her vocation to the priesthood. 'During her illness, whenever we were cutting her hair she would ask for a tonsure, and then joyfully feel it with her hand.' One can only admire the prophetic audacity with which Thérèse

---

* In *St Thérèse of Lisieux — By Those Who Knew Her (Testimonies from the process of Beatification)*, edited and translated by Christopher O'Mahony, Veritas Publications, Dublin 1975 (reprinted 1996), pages 155 and 156.

could take upon herself part of the ordination ritual! Thérèse obviously considered it important to give some concrete outward expression to the vocation she carried in her heart. The shaving of the crown of her head is the tangible sign of what she believed she was: a priest. Thérèse, so totally obedient to God's will, would not have done it if she had not believed that it expressed something of the truth about herself. 'God never gave me a desire that He did not fulfil,' Thérèse had affirmed. Was her tonsure a sign of her ordination by desire, just as one can receive baptism and confirmation by desire, in exceptional circumstances?

It is ironic that one of the medieval theologians referred to in *The Declaration on the Question of the Admission of Women to the Ministerial Priesthood* (Sacred Congregation for the Doctrine of the Faith, 1976) had argued that women could not be ordained because their hair was unsuitable for the tonsure! The Vatican document acknowledges 'that modern thought would have difficulty in admitting or would even rightly reject' some of these arguments. However, these theologians are still adduced in support of 'the constant tradition of the Church'.

Why did Thérèse desire so much to be a priest? The short answer is that she believed that it was a desire that God had planted in her heart. It is certainly not the case that she idealised priests or put them on a pedestal. Whatever illusions in this regard she may have had as a child were completely removed during her pilgrimage to Rome before entering the convent. She discerned very clearly that ordination did not remove any human frailty, and that it was not instant holiness. All her experiences in the convent confirmed this: through her correspondence with two young priests, she was well placed to know how much they needed her prayers.

Thérèse's desire to be a priest, like everything else in her, was motivated by her passionate zeal to share God's love with all. How she longed to be able to preach the Word, to share the insights God had given her! She remarked, 'I have never heard a priest preach properly about God's love!' and 'How I would love to be a priest in order to preach about the Blessed Virgin!' Thérèse, profoundly rooted in the mystery of the incarnation, also longed to preside at the Eucharist. She deeply desired to be able to 'call Him down from Heaven' and 'to hold Him in [her] hands'. Her inspiration and model was Mary, the mother of God. In one of her poems she speaks of 'the priest at the altar like Mary at the foot of the cross', and [elsewhere] she writes, 'O Divine Word ... The ministers of your altars should handle you as lovingly as Mary when she was putting you in your swaddling clothes.'

When Thérèse was alive, no woman saint had ever been proclaimed Doctor of the Church. This particular long-standing tradition of considering women unfit for the role was finally broken in 1970. It is reported that at the time Pope Paul VI was worried that this might be used as a wedge to open the door to women priests, but was reassured by his theologians that this would not happen. I believe that the theologians were wrong, but that the ordination of women is not a cause for worry but for rejoicing. St Thérèse, Doctor of the Church, with her 'boldness', 'unerring judgement' and 'brilliant womanly wisdom' (John Paul II), assures us that a woman can indeed be a priest, for with God nothing is impossible.* And I have no doubt that, when the Church finally catches up with her, she will shower more roses on us all! *Magnificat!*

---

*   Sr Catharina Broome OP, 'The Priestly Vocation of Thérèse of the Child Jesus', in *Spirituality* Vol. 6 Nos. 30 and 31 (Dominican Publications, Dublin).

❧

FATHER MICHAEL MAHER, SM, DUBLIN

I overheard two Dublin women on the way back from visiting the relics saying to each other, 'Ah no, faith is not dead; the only thing is they're not practising!'

I pondered about it afterwards, and concluded, yes — the Holy Spirit is alive and active and continues to whisper softly to us of God's presence within us. There is present that secret, silent longing to love and be loved. In Ireland we must be alert to this and not allow the subtle powers of darkness quench the flame. It is so important to continue to give each other our own space.

During the visit of the relics, many priests were surprised and somewhat humbled at the number of people who availed of the Sacrament of Reconciliation. When some people were asked what it was that encouraged them to come to Confession, the answer invariably was: 'Oh, but Father, it was like a quiet inner voice which just said, "Go to Confession."'

I guess there is a shower of roses whose petals continue to float softly and gently down, telling all of us how much God really loves us.

❧

MARY GALLAGHER, ROSCOMMON

Her young face and the set of her head show spirit, beauty and challenge. She could be the Leaving Certificate pupil who will always ask the awkward question in class that cuts through the pat, learned-by-rote notes. No wonder the young love her, with her sound-bite of 'Love alone counts,' and came in their thousands with roses.

The perennial subjects of death and man's destiny are close to the Irish psyche. An exhibition at the National Museum, some years ago, showed reliquaries heavily decorated in gold that used to be carried into battle by the Picts and Celts: the dead infusing the living with their spirit of courage and faith.

St Thérèse of Lisieux was familiar to me. At home, we had her statue beside the tea caddy, with her cream, brown and black habit and her bunch of roses. A statue was to help meditation, not an object of worship, as we mini-theologians learned. Every crisis was referred to the Little Flower. Where St Patrick might have had an austere Spartan image, and God himself, at that time, was a little forbidding, she was the neighbour's child who would put in a good word. Emigration, loneliness, alcoholism, exams and jobs were all her province. It didn't matter that she was French and that she spoke a different language; there was nothing foreign about her. She was the Little Flower — dependable, approachable, reliable; not soulful, martyred or doe-eyed, but mischievous: a person who could say to God, when he hadn't responded to her, 'Well, if that's the way you treat your friend, no wonder you have so few.'

During the visit of her relics, she made contact with prisoners, soldiers, tenors, dancers, and drug addicts. People from Fair Head in Antrim to Mizen Head in Cork came to venerate her. Ferries and helicopters transported her. Millions of roses were laid down beside her.

John Waters, in 'Writing of Modern Ireland', writes:

> At the centre of the ideology of modern Ireland is a core meaning which has to do with a particular notion of progress. Fundamentally,

this core notion is deeply materialistic, for it has equated improvement of the Irish way of life with economic growth only. This very criticism, although occasionally made by clerics, left-wingers or the generally disgruntled, has almost no credibility on account of the inability of those making it to influence anything. This ideology has now supplanted all others, including the ideology of Christianity which has prevailed for more than a thousand years.

Maybe the very lack of influence of which he speaks was counter-acted in the only way a neutered people could make a statement: witness, presence and veneration.

I went to Clarendon Street church to venerate the relics of St Thérèse. Behind me was an old, wheezing lady with a walking aid, before me young, beautiful teenagers carrying flowers. Businessmen in Hugo Boss suits laid their hands reverently on the reliquary. Young be-sashed men and Carmelite priests kept vigil like Red Branch Knights. What were these old bones to us, in our absurd great leap forward — our inflated property pages, bleached oak floors, laptops and credit cards? Our veneration was a silent, profound, inarticulate acknowledgement of our banished past and a faith put in cold storage. We were a wounded people, in a suffer-ing and lacerated Church, with a hunger reaching back to very old, sturdy roots where we had always found sustenance. Like all the pilgrims who ever preceded us, we were flawed, suffering, dispirited, young, old, bawdy, scholarly, addicted, anarchic, but drawn by the same mystery of transcendence, the sense of the sacred that we almost allowed to perish. As I put my hand on the reliquary, I was connected with the world of faith, hope, prayer and a revitalising link with the past that had neither victory or defeat, only hope and the confidence that generations of the Irish had in the Little Flower.

'Love alone counts.' Indeed it does; and who knows the need of it better than ourselves? Little Flower of Lisieux, pray for us.

❦

SISTER GWEN OF THE HOLY SPIRIT, WICKLOW

Our monastery is situated in the parish of Kilquade, Co. Wicklow. Last 28–29 April we hosted the visit of the reliquary of St Thérèse to our parish.

Afterglow

They flowed like the tall meadow grasses,

Whispering their hungers,

Weary from the fog of tattered searching.

You could almost feel the depth of their gaze

On Thérèse

Needing no courage beyond the fire of their longing

For love.

The village said we put the whole thing

Into their hearts

By the glow of our silent presence here.

❦

'I feel in me the vocation of the PRIEST. With what love, O Jesus, I would carry You in my hands when, at my voice, You would come down from heaven. And with what love would I give You to souls! But Alas! While desiring to be a Priest, I admire and envy the humility of St. Francis of Assisi and I feel the vocation of imitating him in refusing the sublime dignity of the Priesthood'
Thérèse of Lisieux

❦

Sister Mary Cecilia, Wicklow

Dry Bones

Dry bones
Encased in a magnificent casket.
Dry bones
Six sturdy men to carry it.
Why? Who? What is its secret?
Mysterious.
Questions not answered by words
But by actions unexpected.
Crowds queuing, thousands thronging,
Old and young, sick and well,
Patiently waiting, fervently praying
In faith and hope and trust,
Inexplicable.
Lost in wonder at the reliquary,
Gazing spellbound, awestruck,
Touching, kissing, kneeling, weeping,
Through the day, all through the night
They come — drawn as by a magnet.
Irresistible.
Listen! These dumb dry bones speak,
And in their dead immobility
Point beyond themselves.
'We are but an icon, no more, no less,
Reaching out towards the Transcendent
God of Love and Mercy.
Go to Him.'

❦

JACK HYNES, MAYO

When I heard that the relics of Thérèse of Lisieux were being brought around Ireland, my first reaction was negative. Was this another attempt to re-energise the 'old institutions' while avoiding the real conversion and the real change that were needed in the Irish Church?

Nevertheless, when it was announced that the relics were being brought to the Carmelite monastery in Knock, Co. Mayo, I found myself going there to pay my respects. When I came back I asked myself, why did I go? What did Thérèse mean to me?

For many years now, I have had the privilege of working with people in recovery from addiction. I have been granted the privilege of sharing, in a small way, their painful road towards recovery. The 'one-day-at-a-time' Twelve-Step Programme is simplicity itself, but it is also heroic! All those who succeed in maintaining their sobriety must commit themselves to a spiritual programme. Essentially, that is what AA is about.

The life and spiritual way of Thérèse shares similarity to the AA programme. She played down the heroism of her spiritual way by calling it the 'Little Way'. Thérèse brought a refreshing perspective to the spiritual way of life at a time when the path to perfection had been 'privatised' and belonged to the élite. The spiritual methods and systems had become the property of specialists — the Benedictines, Franciscans, Carmelites and Jesuits, etc. They were no longer available to the ordinary Christian.

Then along comes this sickly, frail young woman who revolutionised our approach to the Divine. She claimed that she was unable to follow these lofty methods and could only always be in the kindergarten class of the great spiritual masters. When she fell asleep during meditation, she excused herself. When she felt unable to do any great penance or recite long prayers, she expected to be understood and forgiven. She seemed to have no high ambition to perform great spiritual deeds. Her God did not tabulate merits and demerits.

Thérèse radiated a gratitude for life. She played down the profound heroism of her simple spiritual way. She went unnoticed among her contemporaries — nothing spectacular. It was something that the ordinary Christian might try to follow and put into practice in their own lives.

As I sat there, with other people from teenagers to grannies, we sat quietly together in the presence. Still others brought a single rose to lay near the casket. There was no great sense of awe — just a warmth and a welcome that embraced you. People seemed to be saying 'Thanks' to her for the grace of her coming. It was as if they were saying, 'You're one of our own.'

Thérèse taught us all that, whatever hand of cards we are dealt, we must be grateful and play them to the best of our ability. The ultimate gift is the gift of life itself. When we give thanks for this gift, we say it all. Thérèse gave thanks for her life, even her illness.

While uncertain in the beginning whether I should go or not, on reflection I am grateful I went to sit in her presence. The visit reminded me to be grateful for life — and hopefully will teach me to say 'Thanks' for the vehicle of my departure.

❀

Don Mullan

MARGARET O'NEILL, WICKLOW

Give Me the Heart of a Child

Give me, O Lord, the heart of a child,
Simple and joyful and free.
Give me, O Lord, the love of a child,
Trusting and faithful to Thee.
Don't let my age make a difference, Lord,
If I'm middle-aged, young or old;
What matters is that I've the heart of a child,
Simple and pure as gold!
Yes, simple and pure as gold, dear Lord,
That's tried in the furnace of fire;
Oh! then let me have the heart of a child
And I'll have achieved your desire.
For how often in Gospel stories
You gathered the little ones near,
And you begged all the adults about,
'Be childlike and have no fear!'
For fear drives out love, dearest Lord,
And You've asked us to be meek and mild.
And therefore I beg You, my Master,
Please give me the heart of a child!

(first published in *Ireland's Own*, June 2001)

❁

MAY McCLINTOCK, DONEGAL

[I am] a member of the Church of Ireland. I first heard of St Thérèse when a friend staying here had a copy of her biography. I reread it this year — it would have been difficult not to be aware of the visit, being very much a media story which caught the popular imagination.

I went to Letterkenny Cathedral twice — first of all to watch the arrival, and later I joined the long queue in the late evening. To try to analyse the reasons: perhaps to be part of a community celebration, a sense of the historical occasion.

I touched the reliquary and admired the casket, which was even more beautiful than portrayed in photographs. I cannot adequately describe how I felt at the time — perhaps something similar to how I feel when I join the congregation in Roscrea Abbey on Easter Eve, or my first view of Loch Derg. My abiding memory will be the silence: no one spoke or whispered, people seemed to be unaware of those around them, everyone seemed to be alone in their thoughts. To make eye contact with an acquaintance would have been an invasion of their private reflections.

I have heard comments about allowing St Thérèse rest in peace, but she did ask to be taken to the corners of the world. Am I right that Jesus commanded his disciples to go out and preach the Gospel? Surely St Thérèse is our modern disciple.

❀

SISTER MAIRÉAD BROPHY, DUBLIN

> *Jesus and Thérèse*
> On a day full of love
> he became small,
> so small
> only another child would play with him;
> so he gave himself to her.
> Yes, he gave himself,
> so fully, so real.
> And she gave herself,
> at a different time,
> in a different place,
> to him,
> so fully, so real,
> love ebbing and flowing
> between.

❦

MICHAEL O'CONNOR, CORK

I first heard of St Thérèse through a very dear friend of my wife, Mary. Joe Heffernan, a computer instructor, came to help Mary with her ECDL course.

I had been writing creatively during the previous two years, and recently had approached Eddy Lyons, editor of *Inside Cork*. In the end he asked me to write on events in Cork City. That was the previous Friday.

When Joe had finished helping Mary we all sat down for coffee. As Joe began to explain his own profound experiences of St Thérèse, her life and the importance of her visit to Ireland, I felt this was going to be one big story. I took out a dictaphone and asked Joe to speak. I could see, hear and feel this man's sincerity and pride as he spoke. He had a reverence and without doubt a love for this woman and the life of suffering this little French nun had lived. I sat in awe of him.

I got in touch with my editor next morning, and he asked for four hundred words on Thérèse and the visit. This was my first article and I was very excited. Within twenty-four hours I had sent in my first article, on the life of a young woman whom I had never heard of before. It was the beginning of my freelance writing career.

I was enraptured with the story of Thérèse as I found out more about her life. I would go to her altar frequently to pray and ask for guidance. I identified with Thérèse's own problems and her great belief in Our Lady's smile that gave her clarity in her own mind. I was taken by Thérèse's privileged background — the fact that she came from a wealthy background and yet she left it all behind her for a very simple life in the convent. I came from a well-off family and I was educated in two private boarding schools; now I live a different life, and my philosophy now is 'less is more'. But during the last few years I have developed a great trust, which Thérèse had in her philosophy that Providence does provide.

On the morning of Thérèse's arrival in Rosslare, my friend Joe Heffernan and I left Cork at 4.15 a.m. to get there on time. As the day unfolded, it was with certainty I felt I was in the places that mattered. I unwittingly ended up on the ramp of the ferry, and as the reliquary was escorted down the ramp I got my first sight of the enormity of what St Thérèse was about. As the reliquary passed in front of me I felt a presence that made me hold my breath.

My most memorable event on the visit was my inclusion as a reporter to Mountjoy Jail for Thérèse's visit there. I was one of a handful of reporters to cover the event. I was definitely privileged. That night in the Dóchas Centre at Mountjoy Women's Prison, I saw what a sense of Thérèse meant to the women here.

The jail was spotless. There was a great welcome from Assistant Governor Catherine Comerford and from Chaplain Father Eamon Crossan, who earnestly spoke of his work to me, but it was the warmth and pride of the women prisoners present that really won me over. The hall was beautifully decked out with posters, flowers and paintings. The women, all dressed casually, had worked together with staff and the community to create a special welcome for Thérèse. Thérèse had a devotion to prisoners, particularly with the repentance of Frenchman Henri Pranzine, a triple murderer, in 1887. I felt I was witnessing something very private and sensitive, a form of grace and a kind of metamorphosis. When I left the prison that night, I was more afraid of what was out there than of what I had left behind in Mountjoy.

As Thérèse left by helicopter from the GAA grounds in Wexford, it was with mixed emotions I waved goodbye. It had all been written. It had all been said. I was saying goodbye to a friend, someone whom I cared for. She had taken on an almost living presence for me. There was almost a grieving, a loss. I felt Thérèse had taken care of me.

❀

FATHER DAMIAN MCNEICE, DUBLIN

(Homily preached during a Mass in St Joseph's Carmelite Monastery, Seapark, Malahide, on 2 May, whilst the relics were there)

It is right and good that we should honour the relics of St Thérèse. The glory, light and beauty of Christ's love shone very brightly in and through her body. And now she has masterminded a way to use her mortal remains, her relics, to catch more souls into the love of God. She said she always wanted to be a missionary, 'a fisher of souls'. She is getting her way. As a wise priest once said to me, 'Never cross a Carmelite nun.'

The sub-prioress in the Carmel of Lisieux described the twenty-year-old Thérèse's life thus: 'A little goody-goody to whom you would give Communion without sending her to Confession, but as artful as a wagonload of monkeys. She can make you weep with devotion and just as easily faint with laughter during recreation.'

When Thérèse was a little child, her mother was worried about her, and she wrote: 'As for the little ferret, I don't know how she is going to turn out.... When she says no, nothing will change her.' When Thérèse grew up and wanted to say 'Yes' to her Beloved, her Jesus, nothing too would change her. As she wrote: 'I want to love, to love Love and make Love loved.' You could almost see that as her motto.

Carmelite priest Father Ian Matthew, speaking about Thérèse, once said, 'Little Flower? More like the Big Thistle, if you ask me!' She had an iron will, the will of a soldier or a warrior. She was passionately in love with Jesus; she wanted to possess him and be possessed by him completely.

Thérèse brings us back to Gospel values. Jesus said, 'Love one another as I have loved you.' Thérèse realised that, for us, this is impossible — unless we allow the Lord come live in us, pray in us, work through us, breathe in us, love through us. As she said, 'My love, Lord, in comparison to yours is something less than a drop of dew lost in your ocean. How do I love you as you love me? The only way to do that is to come to you for the loan of your own love.' She understood that if that drop of dew surrenders itself, plunges into the ocean, it becomes one with the ocean; and so she went on this path of abandonment and surrender.

At that time, there was a strong influence in the Church from guilt-ridden spirituality called Jansenism, and people even inflicted suffering on themselves, believing that would bring them closer to God. They practised what could be a false perfectionism. Thérèse felt that there was no sense in mortifying yourself if you can't put up with the everyday pins and needles of having to put up with each other. There was, for example, one Sister in the community — Sister Augustine; Thérèse wrote of her, 'There is a Sister in the community who rubs me up the wrong way at every turn. I find her manner, her speech, her character, very disagreeable. I know that God must love her dearly.... I am determined to treat her as if she were the person I loved best in the world.' One day this Sister came up to Thérèse and said, 'Sister Thérèse, what is it that attracts you so much to me? Every time you see me you have a smile for me.' And poor Thérèse didn't have the heart to tell her that what was attracting her was 'Jesus hidden in the depth of her soul'. And there was also Sister Joseph — a gifted but difficult person, whom Thérèse described as being 'like an old clock that has to be wound up every quarter of an hour'. We may laugh at this; but, remember, Thérèse did the winding. There is the Gospel in practice.

Thérèse didn't waste energy worrying about past sins. One phrase that I especially like from her is where she says of God: 'He is Love and Mercy — that is all.' She understood how God delights in stooping down to lift us out of our own shame, weakness, sinfulness, just like the most tender parent would help a baby out of its own dirt, upset and mess. So Thérèse invites us to acknowledge our littleness, our own poverty of love, and to abandon ourselves to God's will, because there is no more loving way than God's way. She invites us into the way of total confidence, trust with God, just as a child looks to a parent for all that it needs.

One image Thérèse used time and time again in her writings to describe this love is that of a flame, a fire, a furnace. But what happens when you put rubbish on a fire? It doesn't put it out; it burns even brighter. Thérèse understood that that's what happens when we throw our sins onto the furnace of God's love for us.

She had a special place in her heart for those whom she called 'materialists'. I suppose she had a very good lesson for those of us to live in the time of the Celtic Tiger. She made herself sister to all those who had lost their bearings, those who were hopeless, despairing, atheist, those who have lost meaning in their lives — especially in the last eighteen months of her life, when she herself was plagued with doubts about the existence of a Heaven. Therefore she identified herself in solidarity with those who cannot believe.

Remember, her religious name is St Thérèse of the Child Jesus and of the Holy Face. She joined herself so much to her Jesus, her suffering spouse, that she offered herself in union with Him in atonement for sinners. In contemplating the Holy Face of Jesus in His Passion, she saw that it is, in a mysterious way, Godlike and

Christ-like to suffer, and that suffering, united with the Cross of Jesus by His power, can heal and redeem and save. This is her greatness, this is her message to us and to our age — because she entered into the absence of God, the forgetfulness of God, the deforestation of our culture of its Christian language and meaning, that is so much part of our world today.

Isn't it amazing that a girl who entered a Carmelite convent at fifteen, and who died unknown aged twenty-four, could explode so much onto the scene? Surely, this is a sign that God is at work powerfully here.

One of Thérèse's favourite lines in Scripture was from a beautiful book in the Old Testament called the Song of Songs, where it says, 'Draw me and we will run.' In asking the Lord to draw her closer, she understood that the Lord would also be drawing all of those who were tied to her heart by bonds of affection. Through our honouring of you this day, Thérèse, may the Beloved draw us. Help us to run with you with trust into the embrace of God — that embrace of God who, you were and are certain, is 'more tender-hearted than any mother'.

❦

SISTER ISABELLE SMYTH, MEDICAL MISSIONARIES OF MARY, DROGHEDA, CO. LOUTH

Their dates of birth were separated by only nineteen years. Marie Françoise Thérèse Martin would never know of Marie Helena Martin, at least not on this Earth. But she was destined to have a major influence on the life of Marie Helena — the woman who would one day become the Foundress of the Medical Missionaries of Mary.

Marie Françoise Thérèse was born on 2 January 1873, the youngest of nine children of Louis Martin and Zélie Guérin of Alençon, France. This devout couple had known great loss. A little daughter had died at the age of four-and-a-half; another died when only three months old. The couple dearly desired a son who might become a priest and a missionary; for this they prayed fervently. But their son died at the age of five months. Another son was born, but he flew off to Heaven at the age of nine months.

When they brought their last baby to be christened, they could hardly have imagined that one day she would announce that she wanted to become a priest. But that was an idea the Church would find difficult to accept.

Sorrow was never far from the Martin household. Zélie developed cancer. She bore this suffering for years until her death, on 28 August 1877. She was forty-seven years old.

Little Marie Françoise Thérèse was not yet five. She later wrote about the loss of her mother, 'My happy disposition completely changed, I became timid and retiring, sensitive to an excessive degree....' Attacks of scruples and anxiety would come later.

Louis Martin felt the heart had gone out of their Alençon home. He moved the family to Lisieux.

When she was nine, Thérèse suffered a prolonged serious illness. No treatment helped. One day, she turned to a statue of the Virgin Mary near her bed and prayed for a cure. 'Suddenly,' Thérèse wrote, '... Mary's face radiated kindness and love.' She knew she had been cured. The statue has since been called Our Lady of the Smile.

The story of how Thérèse wanted to become a Carmelite but was too young is well known. In 1887, when her father took her and her sister Céline on pilgrimage to Rome, she defied all protocol: during the audience with Pope Leo XIII, she ran to his feet and cried out, 'Most Holy Father, I have a great favour to ask you! In honour of your jubilee, permit me to enter Carmel at the age of fifteen.'

'Well, my child,' the Holy Father replied, 'do what the superiors tell you.'

Thérèse made a final plea: 'Oh, Holy Father, if you say yes, everybody will agree!' She later wrote: 'He gazed at me steadily, speaking those words and stressing each syllable: "Go — go — you will enter if God wills it."' On New Year's Day 1888, the Prioress of the Lisieux Carmel advised Thérèse she would be received into the monastery the following April.

Thérèse perceived her life's mission as one of salvation for all. She thought of herself as the new Joan of Arc, dedicated to the rescue not only of France, but of the whole world. Her spirituality was grounded in love, and in a deep faith that what God wanted was never impossible.

Marie Françoise Thérèse died on 30 September 1897, having suffered greatly from tuberculosis. She was only twenty-four years old. She was canonised on 17 May 1925 by Pope Pius XI; she was named Co-Patron of the Missions in 1927, and became the third woman Doctor of the Church in 1997.

In Dublin, Ireland, Marie Helena was born on 24 April 1892, the second of twelve children of Thomas Martin and Mary Moore. Marie developed rheumatic fever in 1904, after a drive home during a snowstorm. This was to leave her with a legacy of heart trouble and ill health that dogged her throughout her life.

This Martin family also knew sorrow. On St Patrick's Day in 1907, when Mary Martin was pregnant with her twelfth child, her husband Thomas died from a gunshot wound, believed to be accidental. The bond between Marie and her mother grew even closer after that.

When war broke out in 1914, Marie trained for the Voluntary Aid Detachment and was posted first to Malta and later to France. When the war was over, Marie Helena returned home, matured by the things she had seen. In 1921, at the age of twenty-nine, she went to Nigeria as a lay missionary. The situation she encountered quickly convinced her that single-handed she could do little. To make any impact, she would have to establish a congregation of committed religious women trained in medicine, surgery and obstetrics.

But that was an idea the Church would find difficult to accept. Besides, few universities would allow women into medical school in the early 1920s. These obstacles did not cause her to doubt her calling. She was guided by a deep belief that 'If God wants the work, God will show the way.'

Yet, in 1927, it seemed impossible that the calling she felt so deeply could be followed in her lifetime. Mindful of the missionary role of the recently canonised St Thérèse, she thought she might follow the way of Carmel instead. She sought admission to the Carmelite convent in Hampton, Dublin. Although she received all the votes of the community, the Prioress, Mother Dympna, was convinced that her vocation was not to Carmel.

Marie Helena had to wait until 1936 before the Church acknowledged the value of religious women in the practice of surgery and obstetrics. When she made her vows, on 4 April 1937, she was gravely ill in a government hospital in Nigeria. She took the name Mother Mary of the Incarnation. When she was well enough, the doctor advised that she take the first ship back to Ireland.

In 1949, she made a visit to Lisieux, where she told the Prioress — St Thérèse's sister Pauline (Mother Agnes) — about the history of MMM, with its many ups and downs. Mother Agnes promised 'to see to it that my holy sister Thérèse will answer all your petitions and the intentions of your friends and benefactors, and obtain all that your congregation needs'.

Mother Agnes presented Mother Mary with a stone from the wall of the convent infirmary where St Thérèse had died — a gift to be used as a foundation stone for the new hospital that Mother Mary hoped to build in Drogheda. Mother Agnes added a prayer that the saint would adopt the entire MMM congregation, 'showing herself ever a sister to the MMMs, labouring in and through them, and spending her Heaven doing good with them on Earth'.

These Martin girls were women of their time. Their writings and spirituality were informed by the language and theology of that time. To the mind-set of today, that can appear out of date; but the courage of these women in overcoming personal difficulties and external obstacles does not become dated. Their determination to follow their dream, no matter what the cost, will inspire people in every age.

At noon on Monday, 21 May 2001, the reliquary of Saint Thérèse departed from the mother house of MMM in Drogheda, where it had been venerated by twenty thousand people during the previous twenty-two hours. The cortège paused for just a moment at the entrance to Our Lady of Lourdes Hospital, where the stone from the infirmary where Thérèse died is embedded beneath the altar. Just to the right, in St Peter's Cemetery, is the tomb of Marie Helena Martin, who died on 27 January 1975. It was, indeed, a profound moment.

JOE MCGORIAN, DUBLIN

My Little Soulmate
I have a little soulmate
Who watches over me.
She showers my path with roses;
The thorns, she hides from me.
Whenever I am lonely
Or walking through a maze,
She leads me on her Little Way,
My little flower, Thérèse.
She knows my heart was broken;
Hers was broken too.
Love was her calling
And love brought her through.
She is my little soulmate
For the rest of my days,
Till the Good Lord introduces me
To my little flower, Thérèse.

❀

MALACHY TOAL, ARMAGH

When it was announced that the relics of St Thérèse were coming to Ireland, there was a great sense of joy in the ecclesiastical capital of Ireland. The people of Armagh deemed it a singular privilege that the relics would be visiting our archdiocese, the seat of St Patrick, and our great twin-spired cathedral.

Plans were immediately set in motion for the welcoming of the relics, and a committee of parishioners was set up. As the time drew nearer for the visit, it became obvious that it was going to take a lot of personnel to ensure everything went smoothly. A meeting of the parishioners was called, and the response was magnificent, with over six hundred people signing up to help in the various areas — e.g. stewarding, guard of honour, pallbearing, erecting a shrine to the saint, erecting signs and flags, preparing the cathedral inside and out. It was the greatest response to a request for help that Armagh parish had witnessed in many years.

As 2.00 p.m. on Friday, 25 May, approached, the thirty-nine bells of St Patrick's Cathedral rang out over the city as thousands gathered from throughout the archdiocese. The clouds that had been threatening to bring the previous few days of sunshine to an end held back to allow a golden welcome. On the stroke of 2.00 p.m. the reliquary arrived at the main gates of the cathedral; Bishop Gerard Clifford, Auxiliary to the Archbishop of Armagh, accompanied by clergy of the archdiocese, descended the cathedral steps to greet it.

The procession moved slowly up the Cathedral Avenue, through a guard of honour of hundreds of schoolchildren, to the main door of the cathedral. As the relics, borne on the shoulders of members of the Armagh branch of the Order of Malta, moved towards the main entrance, fifty thousand rose petals showered down from the twin spires of the cathedral, coming to rest over the casket and the steps of the cathedral. The people gasped and then burst into loud applause.

During the twenty-two-hour visit an estimated fifty thousand pilgrims, including many young people and young couples and not a negligible number of Protestants, thronged past the reliquary, to touch, to pray, to spend a moment of silence. Petition slips were available to write a prayer of supplication, and many chose to have a candle lit at the shrine specially erected in the saint's honour, adorned with her beloved roses. The occasion was truly a pilgrimage, with all the attendant graces and blessings.

As required, the stewards would stop the throng to allow the sick and infirm and those with disabilities — who entered through a separate entrance — to spend a few moments beside the relics. To see the smiles on sick little children as they viewed and touched the casket was deeply touching. The visit, indeed, was deeply moving for those of strong and weaker faith alike — and all were privileged to be part of what they could clearly perceive to be a grace-filled and blessed moment.

The visit of the relics of St Thérèse was truly a memorable occasion that touched many people, eased the pain of the sick, gave everyone a sense of hope, and, indeed, for some marked a new beginning. It was a feast of colour and music, a festival of faith and joy. May peace of mind and heart and a renewed faithfulness to the Gospel be the long-term legacy of the visit. With the help of St Thérèse, may we become ever more perfect images of the love of God. May the intentions for which so many prayers were offered, so many petitions written and so many candles lit, through the intercession of the Little Flower, be answered.

❧

EMMA, NIAMH AND KATRINA LENNON (AGED 14, 17 AND 19)

'I Shall be Love'
(Saint Thérèse)

I shall be love;
A thousand proofs, O Lord,
Of my love
I give to you in every little thing I do.
In every little way I shall be love.

I shall be yours
In every little way,
Completely yours;
So trustingly I step towards your arms,
And there I lay me down.
I always will be yours.

And oh, how this confidence will guide me
Like a child too tiny for concern,
Like a dream — someday I will waken,
And what joy is waiting there for me!

And then this love,
With blessings, I will send
A shower of roses down to every friend
So they might know my way.
And in that little way,
An ordinary way,
In my little way, there shall be love.

🌹

FATHER JOHN LAWLER O.CARM., KILDARE

It was 4.30 in the morning. People were still coming to venerate the relics of Saint Thérèse: old people shuffling along on sticks; young couples, hand in hand; youths, Nicodemus-like, avoiding the glare and possible mockery of peers. The reverence and silence was palpable as they all touched, even caressed, the reliquary. I wondered what it all meant to each one of them.

Then I remembered something Thérèse had said about her trip to Rome with her father and Céline: 'I always had to find a way of touching everything.' She was talking about holy places and holy things. There was that memorable visit to the Colosseum, when she and her sister Céline crossed the forbidden barrier to find the pavement the guide had spoken of where so many Christian martyrs had shed their blood. Thérèse describes the moment:

> We soon found it and threw ourselves on our knees on this sacred soil, and our souls were united in the same prayer. My heart was beating hard when my lips touched the dust stained with the blood of the first Christians. I asked for the grace of being a martyr for Jesus and felt that my prayer was answered.

In touching the pavement, Thérèse was trying to get in touch with a mystery of love that had been acted out in that place, and she prayed that she might become part of that mystery herself. Touching the pavement had a kind of sacramental value for her.

I felt that something analogous was happening here. Many of these people would have known little about Thérèse, other than the fact that she was a woman of great love. They were trying to get in touch with that mystery of love that was Thérèse, in the hope that they might share in that mystery and have it change and transform their lives. It was unlikely that the majority of them would have been able to articulate that desire for themselves as clearly as Thérèse had done in Rome. But it was there in their deportment, it was there in their reverence, it was there in their reluctance to leave the reliquary and return to the business of the day ahead. Somewhere within them, the Holy Spirit was at work. That same Spirit who helps us to pray with sighs too deep for words was helping them to express in symbol what their minds could hardly conceive. Touching the reliquary was like a little sacrament working on their unconscious depths.

There is no adequate translation from the opaqueness of symbols to the clarity of concepts and words. But I found myself praying for them, that such clarity would come: 'Keep in touch with them, Thérèse, and help them to keep in touch with you by discovering and following your Little Way of Spiritual Childhood and total trust in the Fatherhood of God.'

❧

FATHER ELTIN GRIFFIN O.CARM., DUBLIN

The visit of the relics of St Thérèse to Ireland will go down in history as a totally unique event. Those who threw cold water on the whole idea in the beginning have become silent. Father David Weakliam O.Carm., parish priest of Knocklyon, described their approach as 'an inability to cope with mystery'. We have been present at something unexpected and mysterious. One Irish bishop claimed that it has touched a nerve in a way that no other event during the millennium succeeded in doing. Father Patrick Staunton O.Carm., parish priest of Beaumont, put it very well when he said in an interview, 'It can hardly be put into words.'

Everywhere they rolled out the red carpet for the relics of St Thérèse. Every place was different. There was a terrific sense of welcome at all venues — flags, rose petals, guards of honour, scouts, bands, a piper — and they rang out the bells from the churches of other communions as a gesture of welcome. Celebrating the Church's night prayer of Compline with a chapel full of people at eleven o'clock in Gort Muire on a Sunday night was a foretaste of Heaven, something we may never see again.

What emerges — using the language of the Acts of the Apostles — is that it gave heart to the believers. It showed the human face of the Church. It was an experience of the Christian community at its best. Everywhere volunteers came forward to steward crowds, to stand guard over the relics, to decorate churches, to monitor car parks, to convey wheelchair users in and out of churches, allowing them time to view and touch the reliquary. The Gardaí were outstanding in their willingness to be of service; to them we owe an enormous debt of gratitude. Certain sectors of the Defence Forces came to the fore with generosity of spirit when they were needed. The Knights of Malta, the Red Cross and other agencies were very much to the fore for first aid.

The relics of St Thérèse arrived at Rosslare Harbour, courtesy of Irish Ferries, and were accorded full military honours. From Rosslare through several venues in the diocese of Ferns, Thérèse made her triumphant entry into Ireland and took over the country.

Starting out with eighty official venues, the pilgrimage of the relics covered one hundred and twelve in total. Every place was a highlight in its own way. As the relics arrived in Armagh Cathedral, rose petals were dropped from the towers — an amazing sight. The shot on the television screen of the sanctuary in Carlow Cathedral was hauntingly beautiful, with the images of Thérèse in the fore-front. They queued throughout the night at Mullingar Cathedral, as they did in many other places. At Avila Retreat House in Donnybrook, in Terenure College and in Whitefriar Street, Dublin, people were seen stealing in at all odd hours during the night. In the Carmels of Kilmacud, Delgany, Tallow, New Ross, Malahide, Roebuck, Hampton and Firhouse, Carmelite nuns kept vigil at night.

The Carmelite priory at White Abbey, Kildare, is not a very large place; but, according to the Gardaí, 120,000 people passed through in the course of two days. The procession up the Falls Road in Belfast from St Peter's Cathedral to the Redemptorist church at Clonard was a sight to behold, as was the night vigil in the Passionist church at Ardoyne. Father Hugh Kennedy, parish priest of the neighbouring Parish of the Sacred Heart, Old Park, preached a powerful homily. All night long they kept coming.

Sligo Cathedral excelled in the adornment of church and sanctuary. The centrepiece was a huge ball of fire at the end of the altar steps, surrounded by mountains of white lights and roses. Incense wafted upwards and outwards from several corners in the church. Galway Cathedral mounted a youth celebration at midnight, drawing on folk groups from all over the diocese; it was most heartening to see young people present Thérèse in words and music. Music was to the fore again in St John's Cathedral, Limerick, with a different choir or folk group taking over every hour throughout the night. St Mary's Cathedral, Killarney, mounted a brief prayer service every hour, with a priest and a small group of laity taking the lead. Priests from all over the diocese came to lend a hand, and Confessions lasted into the small hours of the morning, as happened in many other venues. Traffic came to a standstill in several towns and villages as the relics passed through. Bishop John Magee held a very gracious and heart-warming reception in Cobh Cathedral; the Naval Cadets formed a guard of honour. Falcarragh, in the heart of the Donegal Gaeltacht, had young girls dressed as Carmelite nuns to lead the parade of welcome; TG4 was very visible, as it was in all Irish-speaking areas. 'Hanging out of the rafters' was the expression used to describe the waiting crowd in Thurles.

Monaghan Cathedral was swamped; twenty thousand prayer leaflets, distributed free of charge, had disappeared by midnight. Heavy rain in the west, in Ballina and Ballaghadereen, did not prevent the crowds turning out. It was the same story everywhere: in Loughrea, Waterford, Letterkenny, Kilkenny, Cork, Longford, Castlemartyr, Ennis, Bruckless in Co. Donegal, and Mount Merrion in Dublin — repeat performances of a joyous reception, beautifully decorated churches, roses everywhere and a great sense of community. Malahide Golf Course put their buggies at the disposal of those leading in the elderly and the infirm. And, would you believe, the shops in Malahide closed up for two hours to give people an opportunity of joining in the welcome parade! A feature unique to Dublin's Pro-Cathedral was the singing of the Litany of St Thérèse to music composed by Father Pat O'Donoghue. Knock Shrine was very special; the Carmelite nuns had a whole twenty-four hours and the shrine two whole days.

Derry City had two bites of the cherry: at St Eugene's Cathedral and at Termonbacca Retreat House, where Bishop Séamus Hegarty preached a most moving homily with a lovely touch of humour.

Newry Cathedral and the Cooley Peninsula are not to be forgotten: the Cooley people who had suffered in the foot-and-mouth outbreak showed their love for Thérèse by erecting a permanent outdoor shrine. Pilgrims present at Lough Derg on 28 June were privileged to have Thérèse arrive in their midst by helicopter. The Carmelite church in Kinsale mounted an ecumenical welcome.

Those who accompanied the relics were overwhelmed by the reception on the part of prisoners in Mountjoy, Cork and Limerick. Even the most rejected came forward to pay their respects and to pray. St James's Hospital in Dublin mounted a magnificent floral display in the church, the members of staff contributing over two thousand pounds. And those unable to leave the wards were not forgotten.

Inevitably, I will have left out some places. I could not possibly include all. Those who first thought up the idea of a Pilgrimage of Grace, as they called it and promoted it, deserve untold thanks — Father J. Linus Ryan O.Carm., Bishop Brendan Comiskey and Father Eugene McCaffrey OCD.

❦

SISTER GABRIELLE MORGAN, DOWN

What is the phenomenal response to the visit of the relics saying to modern Ireland and a wounded Church?

Having lived for over three-quarters of a century, I have been very conscious of the influence of St Thérèse in my own life and locality (Carmelite Convent, Glenvale, Newry).

Over the years, there has evolved in our country (in a world context) a growing sophistication brought about by a pseudo-sense of achievement and dependence on materiality. Alongside this is an ever-growing dissatisfaction and disillusionment in the failure of materialism and empty promises to satisfy hearts and minds. In these days, also, there is a yearning in the hearts of our people to 'search the Scriptures' for a 'way to go'.

However, we long to see the Christ-life embodied in a real flesh-and-blood person of our own times — a person in the ordinary, everyday existence that we know. St Thérèse lived this humdrum life, with its highs and lows — ranging from, and impinging on, issues from the most complex to the deceptively simple.

The message of her life is devoid of the complicated concepts and high-sounding words which many Church people indulge in — often to cover up digressions from the Gospel's call to simplicity, to trust, to love. Thérèse proclaims the truth of the Gospel: it is love which has to be at the heart of the Church — an authentic, universal, integrating love. Wherever hearts hear that call, Thérèse will be welcomed.

❦

GARY WHITE DEER, OKLAHOMA

Some time ago, my friend Don Mullan commissioned me to paint a Native American interpretation of St Thérèse of Lisieux for a book he was writing. I was then involved in organising a Native American dance troupe to tour Ireland on behalf of children at risk in the North and in the Republic. Coincidentally, a fellow organiser, Gemma Jordan of Donabate, assured me that St Thérèse was standing over our little dance troupe project and was watching over me as well. Unknown to me, Gemma had asked St Thérèse to show me a sign that this was so, through the gift of a rose. On my first day in Dublin, my host, Marty Treacy, took me on a tour of her garden and spontaneously presented me with a single rose of the variety known as 'Scented Cloud'. Both Marty and I were very surprised to later learn from Gemma that this was the sign that she had petitioned for.

After I completed my tour with the Native American dancers, I began the St Thérèse commission at the Treacys' home in Donabate. The painting was slow going at first, and I particularly found the likeness of St Thérèse difficult to capture. Marty, who would pop in regularly to check my progress, made the suggestion to 'mix prayer in your paint'. I took Marty's advice, and walked down the hill to Gemma's house to borrow a framed photo of St Thérèse, as well as a prayer card. Adjacent to the painting I put together a small devotional, consisting of a lamp-table, covered with a Native American cloth mat, with the photo and prayer card upon it. Marty provided a candle and a bouquet of roses cut fresh from her garden.

The first time that I said the Prayer of St Thérèse, I earnestly petitioned for divine guidance. The house was empty, and in the silence that followed I could sense two distinct female personages standing behind me, and I was enveloped by a strong sense of peace and well-being. I knelt for a considerable time, not wishing to move, for I knew that when I rose again the feeling of peace would fade. Afterward I made it a practice to light the candle at my little devotional and say the Prayer of St Thérèse before painting. I completed the remainder of the commission, titled *A Shower of Roses*, in this manner.

The night heavens within the painting represent the universality of St Thérèse, and the circle of eagle feathers behind her are used by Native America to symbolise strength, honour, and divinity.

Thérèse is depicted wearing a modern Choctaw dress whose design was originally acquired from the French, once military allies of the Choctaw. Of interest is that the dress pattern is from the region of Normandy, where St Thérèse lived.

St Thérèse is shown letting fall 'a shower of roses', her promise to intercede for us from Heaven. The light flashing from her fingers represents the spark of the divine that I found through prayer while completing the commission. I hope she is pleased.

🌹

FATHER JIM O'HALLORAN, SDB, DUBLIN

From the start, Thérèse of Lisieux seemed determined to teach me that relationships were of the essence. I can recount two experiences to prove it.

The first happening I do not even remember. The lady it concerned told me about it years later. Seemingly she had asked the saint for a special favour and suggested that someone present her with a flower as a sign that her request had been granted. Some days later, she thought she heard a timid knocking on her front door and went out to check. There she confronted yours truly, aged about two, in a small dress — boys began their lives in girls' clothing in those distant days — standing with my hands behind my back. Withdrawing the hands from that position, I presented her with a flower. The woman laughed long and loud. I presume she was expecting a rose; what she got was a flower that in Kilkenny is commonly known as a piss-a-bed. When I eventually went to school, I learned that the respectable name for the blossom was the dandelion. And I was also to learn later that Thérèse had a mischievous sense of humour!

This woman's name was Hannie. She filled my early years with fond stories of the Little Flower. Fortunately, she also filled me with apples from her enchanted orchard.

The second anecdote relates to my first day at school, and I remember it well. Though brimming with tears all day, I was determined not to cry. On no account did I want to be dubbed a crybaby. Seeing that I was homesick, I suppose, Sister Vigilius and Sister Oliver put me sitting by the fire and gave me a bar of chocolate. And I felt a small pang of triumph at bearing up under duress.

As we were about to go home in the early afternoon, I was approached by Thérèse — not the Little Flower, you understand, but a diminutive wraith-like nun also called Thérèse. That morning I had briefly made her acquaintance in the classroom and liked her straightaway; she oozed kindness. And I was certainly in need of it.

'James,' she now asked, 'did you enjoy your first day at school?'

'Yes, Sister,' I mumbled, taken aback by the 'James'. I was always plain Jim at home.

'I have a gift for you.' She produced a coloured picture of a nun in a brown-and-cream habit; in her hands were a bunch of red roses and a crucifix. She had, I thought, a most beautiful face, and I immediately fell in love with her. To no purpose. As Sister Thérèse went on speaking, I learned that this lovely creature was already dead and in Heaven and was 'patroness' of something called the 'missions' (my vocabulary was advancing in quantum leaps). For one who was destined to spend long spells on the missions, this was an event whose significance was not lost on me in later years. I went home treasuring the picture. Thérèse had gently inserted herself into my consciousness for the first time.

However, as I said above, Thérèse seemed intent on impressing upon me the importance of relationships. There was, of course, love in my home; in a special way I recall a dear grandfather who took me to the Friary Chapel, where I experienced all the wonder of flowers, flickering candles, and incense. Hannie and I were fast friends until she died, and she played no small part in my becoming a priest and missionary. Little Sister Thérèse of the Big Book I have never forgotten either, or the kindness of Sister Oliver and Sister Vigilius.

Thérèse shows by her life that she was well aware of the significance of family, friendship, and community. Despite great sufferings, she enjoyed, and contributed to, tremendous love in her natural family. Again at Carmel she had a positive experience of community, not least because she herself was such a superb community person. And during the last two years of her life she shared an exquisite friendship with Maurice Bellière, a seminarian destined to become a priest and missionary. They never saw each other, except in photographs, but they exchanged twenty-one moving letters. Not surprisingly, therefore, she was able to declare: 'God has seen fit to surround me with love at every moment of my life: all my earliest impressions are of smiles and of endearments.' For her, relationships were charged with the love of God, a love to which she was completely open, a love which she mediated for others. She was, in fact, profoundly challenged by Jesus' command that we love one another as he loved us. On reflection, she realised that this was impossible: the love of Jesus was divine, while ours was merely human. So she came up with the ingenious solution that Jesus must 'loan' us his love, and that each one of us should channel that love to others. In this way we would love sensitively and well.

There has been much speculation regarding the significance of the visit of Thérèse's relics to Ireland. I myself venerated them in Whitefriar Street and was profoundly struck by the dignity and quiet devotion of the throngs of people present. There was not a smidgen of triumphalism. And the prayers and readings echoed of sound theology and spirituality. I noted, too, that people came as families, friends, groups, or lovers, and this communal spirit seemed to transform the chemistry of the whole experience.

On my way in, I had been interviewed by a young reporter for the *Sunday Business Post*. He wondered if too much of a fuss was being made over mere bones. I suggested that we not be dismissive of the material. Our bodies share intimately the joys and travails of our lives. Would it not be only fitting that they, in some way, share in the delights of our eternal destiny?

The significance of the visit? I won't argue as to whether two or three million folk came to venerate the relics. By any reckoning, the turnout was quite extraordinary. And the phenomenon had messages for Church and State alike.

Regarding the State, we could say that Thérèse clipped the claws of the Celtic Tiger; disabused us of the spurious notion that diamonds are forever; sharply reminded us that one thing alone is necessary — our salvation. In other words, the visit loudly proclaimed the primacy of the spiritual in our world. This was salutary, as evidence accumulates of more and more lives being wrecked by greed — to what purpose? Meanwhile, we allow a menacing gap between rich and poor to go on growing.

There was bitter, yet wholesome, medicine for the Church as well. We recall the loving family and community experiences of Thérèse, [which] highlight how indispensable relationships are. I feel, however, that the community dimension to the life of Thérèse has not received sufficient attention. As with much of Western spirituality, devotion to the saint has been privatised and overly personalised. The perspective of Vatican II would certainly challenge this position, and Thérèse, by all accounts, deeply influenced that gathering.

In a lapidary statement, the Council declared that the Church ought to be a community in the image of the Trinity (*Dogmatic Constitution on the Church*, 4). This vision is now being realised on all continents through the growth of small Christian communities. In these small communities the members can love and share intimately, as do the Father, Son, and Spirit. Such sharing is impossible in a parish of thousands, or even in a gathering of a hundred. It is done in groups of eight, give or take a couple, that then network with other small communities, in a parish or some such entity, to form a communion of communities. It was noted at an International Consultation on Small Christian Communities in Cochabamba, Bolivia, 1999, that these communities constituted a sleeping giant that, if mobilised, could be a powerful force for good on earth. The participants at the consultation resolved to try and communicate this to bishops everywhere.

Yet many people, instead of looking forward with this vision, look back to the old days of a burgeoning clerical army and crammed seminaries. They are longingly waiting for *fadó* — times past — and are convinced that the fervour surrounding the visit of Thérèse will herald a return to former glories. In vain. I frankly believe that there is no way back for the top-down, institutional Church that we have known. It is now the old Ford car that has had its day, but has no place on our headlong motorways. I feel, too, that it has been fatally wounded by scandals and lack of openness. Besides, there is an inherent difficulty in something that is top-down ever becoming community.

On the contrary, I do think there is a future for a low-profile community model. In it all members, equal through baptism, would participate fully as a priestly people in the life of the Church, not least in the area of decision-making. In this context, the small Christian communities — though not a panacea for all ills, nor the sole instruments for relating people and doing good — could humbly play a constructive role. The proponents of such a model would surely take a radical look at priesthood with a view to reforming it.

The visit of Thérèse, then, challenged us profoundly, yet encouraged and filled us with great hope too.

❦

BISHOP BRENDAN COMISKEY

'What does the visit of the relics of St Thérèse mean to you?' RTÉ's Gerry Ryan asked a young woman on his 2FM morning programme. 'Quite simply, I will have to change my life,' she answered. There was no hysteria and superstition in that, surely — just conversion!

There are two levels on which a response to this grace-filled event can be expected: the level of the individual, and the level of the Church.

If, as has been estimated, three million people came out to venerate the relics at more than one hundred venues, then we can expect three million different responses. Any attempt to capture or categorise these personal responses will have only partial success, but this should not stop us from trying. Some came out of curiosity; others visited the relics simply because they 'went along' with others who were keen on doing so. Some came because their parents or grandparents had a great devotion to the Little Flower, and seemed to experience in the event a kind of communion with these dead relatives. There were those at the various centres who had prayed frequently throughout their lives to the saint and now wanted to visit her 'in person', as they put it.

I had the great privilege of attending at several venues, and the memory I will always have is the expressions on the faces of the people approaching the reliquary. It was a mixture of pain and expectation, of joy shining through tears. So many carried in their hearts and minds the pain and sufferings of others whom they longed to see helped and blessed by St Thérèse. I was deeply moved, particularly when parents and relatives held up little children — especially handicapped children — to see and to touch the reliquary, and found myself hoping and praying that their faith would be rewarded.

My own wish was to sit wordless in the presence of sheer goodness, to be enveloped in God's love, and to do what St John the Evangelist in his first Letter begged us to do: 'Think of the love that the Father has lavished on us, by letting us be called God's children — and that is what we are.' I am utterly convinced that love — God's love for us, not our love for God — must be the starting point of all that we are and do as individuals and as a Church.

The Little Flower's life is above all a story of a soul's confidence in God, trust in God, surrender to God. But how few lives are characterised by these qualities! Why is this? It is because we don't or can't accept that God loves each one of us. Too often we see God as a judge — a just judge, indeed, but still a judge. Some respect judges, others fear them, but I have never met many — apart from their families and friends — who love them! Still fewer feel loved by them! For whatever reason, we have been led to, or choose to, believe that God is Judge rather than Father.

The starting point of St Thérèse's 'Little Way', itself a great gift from God, was her realisation that God loved her for no particular reason or action on her part. She was fascinated by the passage in the Bible where the writer gave as the reason why Jesus chose particular people to follow him, 'He went up the mountain and he took with him those whom he wanted.' Not the holy, not the unholy, not the brightest, not the dumbest — simply those whom he wanted. A journey that doesn't start out from a belief that 'God loves me' is doomed to end up some kind of cul-de-sac.

A second feature of an authentic Theresian journey is that, very often, it starts out from some kind of breakdown or sense of failure. This might be, for example, the experience of the prodigal son in the Bible, who found himself in a pigsty, literally and metaphorically. Life had become a mess. Then came the crucial part: 'He began to think of his father's love.' In other words, he did exactly what St John would later tell the followers of Christ to do: 'Think of the love that the Father has lavished on us, by letting us be called God's children — and that is what we are.'

Or it could be the experience of the young woman on the Gerry Ryan show: 'I simply must change my way of life.' The great tragedy is that when this call to 'come home' or to 'change my life' comes, it is seldom recognised for what it is — namely, a call from God and to God. We think it is some kind of solution to a problem of our own, whereas it is God's invitation. To realise this is a very great grace. If we come to know and appreciate that God is calling us, we will be given all the graces we need along the way.

What should be the response of the Church and of the leaders of the Church to the visit? The greatest mistake of all would be to fail to ask the question: why did three million people visit the relics of

St Thérèse of Lisieux? It would be unwise to ignore the experience of these people and attempt to get back to Church business as usual, especially when it is becoming more and more obvious that a 'business as usual' pastoral strategy is emptying churches of worshippers and people's lives of God.

The real question was never about what was in St Thérèse's reliquary but about what was, and is, in the hearts of people who came in their millions looking for something. Jesus' first question to his first followers was: 'What do you want? What are you looking for?' In modern terminology, we might say that the Lord himself undertook a needs-assessment exercise with his disciples.

It is all about trusting the people, and trusting the Holy Spirit working in their hearts. We must try to ask, and get answers to, the question: 'Why did the largest number of Irish people in the history of this land come out to venerate the relics of St Thérèse at more than one hundred venues in every diocese on this island? What were/are they looking for? What did they find? Are they finding that for which they long in the churches every Sunday — or ever?'

We must — and, I hope, will — use the best scientific research instruments to assist us in the task. This is too great an opportunity to let slip away.

We are indebted to Don Mullan for sharing with us the story of so many people. It is a story that fires the imagination and jump-starts the heart. This is a record of the Holy Spirit breathing where (s)he will throughout our land. It will do hearts good to visit and revisit these pages and be helped to tell our own story of those grace-filled days in the summer of 2001.

'... *truth always wins out.*'
Thérèse of Lisieux

Epilogue

'Forgiveness is the fragrance that the violet sheds
on the heel that has crushed it.'

— Mark Twain

In the immediate aftermath of the attacks on New York and
Washington on Tuesday, 11 September 2001, it was almost impossible for journalists — other than those of the major US networks
— to get into Ground Zero, where the Twin Towers of the World
Trade Center once stood. However, six days after the moment when
history split and a new era of global insecurity dawned, I walked
through Ground Zero, one of the first non-American journalists to
do so. The extraordinary circumstances which culminated in a
literal pilgrimage through New York's valley of tears began with a
chance reference to this book.

During the late afternoon of Monday, 17 September, I travelled
by ferry to the edge of Ground Zero in lower Manhattan. I was with
a close friend, Todd Allen, who works at the Mercantile Exchange at
the World Financial Center. After Todd had caught the last ferry to
New Jersey from the pier close to where he worked, my plan was
to walk along the Hudson to 14th Street and then cross over to the
East Side.

The previous Thursday I had received press accreditation from
the New York Police Department. However, along with other

journalists from Australia, Japan and throughout the US, I was told in no uncertain terms that Ground Zero was out of bounds. A young female officer firmly warned that if we violated police lines the accreditation would be withdrawn and we faced being arrested.

As Todd's ferry carved a white-water trail just north of the Statue of Liberty, I admired a beautiful sunset hanging over the New Jersey skyline. It projected a warm orange hue on the west-facing façades of the surviving skyscrapers on lower Manhattan. As the sun sank the glow crept higher and higher, pulling behind it darkening shadows that made Ground Zero ignite under powerful searchlights. A large pall of smoke rose like a menacing ghost from where there once stood the towering symbols of American stability and opulence. While I could not see into the womb of death, the smell of bombed and burnt-out buildings, well remembered by my senses from the worst days of the 'Troubles' in Derry and Belfast, nullified the familiar smells of New York Harbour.

From my vantage point close to a small marina, I could see nearby skyscrapers, once masterpieces of modern architecture, from which the collapsing towers had torn huge chunks. I could see many charred frames of blackened windows on other buildings; they had been ignited by balls of fire that fell like meteorites after the upper levels of the Twin Towers had swallowed the two hijacked Boeing 767s and been transformed into a holocaust of hatred.

As I stood taking some pictures, scores of firemen and other rescue workers began to exit Ground Zero, walking in my direction. Some were on a break while others, exhausted, had come to the end of another long and distressing day. I was just about to leave when, for no apparent reason, one stopped a few paces beyond me and returned to face me. 'Are you a journalist?' he asked, somewhat sternly.

I began to wonder if I was in trouble, thinking that perhaps I shouldn't be where I was. I answered, 'Yes,' and he asked me whom I worked for. I told him that I was a freelance journalist from Ireland, and that I occasionally wrote for some national papers but my main work involved investigative books and documentaries. I mentioned Bloody Sunday and the Dublin and Monaghan bombings and said I was currently working on a new book about a French saint called St Thérèse of Lisieux.

Immediately his serious countenance vanished and a warm smile of recognition defrosted the moment. 'Our church on Staten Island is named after her,' he said.

His name was Terrence McComiskey, a Senior Special Agent with the US Treasury Department's Bureau of Alcohol, Tobacco and Firearms (ATF). As with the other rescue workers, I observed that his face glistened under the temporary lights — powered by several droning generators somewhere in the background — along the pathway where we stood. He removed his helmet and wiped his brow, his clothing scarred from lifting and hauling mangled metal and broken masonry.

We spoke for a few minutes about the tragedy and the trauma of what lay below the powerful glow beyond the nearby buildings. He talked of the mounting frustrations of all the rescue workers in finding no signs of life. He said that soon their mission would switch from rescue to recovery. Until then, they would continue to work with careful urgency, in the hope of finding even one person alive.

I then asked Agent McComiskey if he knew where St Peter's Church was located, since, if possible, I wished to visit it before returning to Ireland. He was curious about my reasons for wanting to go there. I told him that I had attended the funeral Mass of the Franciscan friar Fr Mychal Judge, Chaplain to the New York Fire Department, two days earlier. Fr Judge's best friend, Fr Michael Duffy OFM, told the congregation that after he had died at the scene of the attack his body was carried to St Peter's Church, where it was laid before the altar. I learned from another Franciscan that Fr Judge had been hit by debris as he gave the last rites to a fellow fire officer — an officer who had, apparently, been felled by the hurtling body of a woman who jumped from somewhere close to the ninety-seventh floor of the North Tower in a desperate effort to escape the merciless inferno.

I told Agent McComiskey that I had been deeply moved by the story of Fr Judge, especially by the esteem in which the New York Fire Department, as well as homeless and marginalised people such as AIDS sufferers, clearly held him. The fact that fire officers collected his body and carried their chaplain to St Peter's was, I felt, an extraordinary act of reverence and devotion. Something within me compelled me to walk in their footsteps and kneel at the altar before which they had laid him.

In addition, my two favourite saints are St Thérèse and St Francis of Assisi. I saw great symbolism in the fact that Fr Judge's remains were the first to be released from Ground Zero.

Agent McComiskey told me that St Peter's Church was located on Barclay and Church Street, just half a block from where the Twin Towers had once stood. In other words, it was located at the epicentre of Ground Zero. He thought for a moment and then suggested we go for a walk. 'If we're stopped, we're stopped,' he said; 'if not, we'll keep walking. Just stay close to me.'

Moving forward, he led me through the darkened concourse of the World Financial Center. Our passage was illuminated by a string of naked bulbs that cast eerie shadows across a restaurant to my right, where dust-covered tablecloths, napkins, cutlery and menus lay abandoned. As we exited through the north entrance, McComiskey drew my attention to an illuminated tent structure, which was a temporary mortuary. He then pointed to a nearby wall against which several rows of brown cardboard boxes were stacked eight feet high, some opened, with black material spilling out. 'There's five thousand body bags there,' he said.

Turning right, we passed near a collapsed pedestrian bridge, and then the full horror of devastation appeared. The scale and dimensions of the destruction are impossible to describe in words. It was both terrifying and traumatising. One understood why there were, and would be, few survivors. The rubble was, by Irish standards, of skyscraper dimensions — six stories above ground and seven below. The rescue workers appeared like an army of ants standing atop the mountain of destruction, seemingly making little or no impact. Thousands of tons of twisted metal, broken girders, miles of limp elevator cables, smashed concrete, shimmering glass fragments from over ninety thousand windows, and a million splinters of what once were desks, doors and shelving, presented the rescuers with a gigantic maze that dwarfed and mocked their heroic efforts.

Almost a week after the attack, smoke still billowed from somewhere underneath. The grey cloud of dust that, in the immediate aftermath of the collapse, had transformed human beings into images of moving statues had by now congealed through heavy rain at the weekend. Everywhere one could see bits of paper that blew across the rubble and nearby streets like confetti. Many carried original signatures on correspondence, contracts and balance sheets — what once was the sweat and toil of the élite corporate community who populated the Twin Towers. Now they were felled and humbled — those giants who, once upon a time, stood as royal sentinels at the gateway of American and world capitalism.

We then came upon World Trade Center 7, which, along with World Trade Centers 3, 4, 5 and 6, had also collapsed. Like a busted accordion, its layers appeared to have fallen forward, spilling like a frozen river into the churning cauldron of death and destruction. Few spoke of this building in the wake of the Towers, but it once stood forty-seven stories high. Smoke also billowed from its highest point, some fifty feet above my head. It was here, at the corner of Vesey and Greenwich Street, that I got the unmistakable sickly-sweet smell of death seeping through the mountains of rubble from several thousand decomposing bodies.

I stood, paralysed by the enormity of the tragedy. Below my grey, mud-clad shoes was the richest piece of real estate in the entire world. The United States of America was the richest nation in the annals of human history. Economically, politically and militarily it stood as the most powerful symbol of invincibility. Billions of tax dollars were spent annually on its armed forces, intelligence-gathering and the development of conventional, biochemical and nuclear weapons. Such spending dwarfed its contribution of development aid to the world's poorest regions. Since coming to power, President Bush had re-ignited the possibility of developing a multi-billion-dollar 'Star Wars' defence system. The United States had gone to war with many enemies, but its theatres had been on the far side of great oceans and on different continents. Its casualties had been brought back in body bags or buried in foreign lands. It had delivered its own horrific payloads of death and destruction throughout the twentieth century. Never, however, even in the darkest days of its War of Independence and Civil War, had it experienced destruction and carnage like this on its own territory.

The devastation I was looking at had been imagined in Hollywood blockbusters such as *Independence Day* and *Deep Impact*, but there it had been caused by fictional aliens from outer space or by earthbound meteorites. This, however, was reality, not Hollywood, and the smell in my nostrils and the churning in my stomach were a universe removed from a comfortable seat with popcorn and Coke. As Terry McComiskey and I continued our journey towards St Peter's Church, straddling the consequences of an evil plot that fundamentalists attempted to masquerade as an act of holy martyrdom, it was clear that a new and frightening era had dawned upon the Earth.

Despite its multi-billion-dollar military prowess, its seventeen and a half miles of Pentagon corridors, its spy satellites and global intelligence networks, no one in the United States government or military saw it coming. And what was most shocking was the simplicity of the plan, executed, almost without a hitch, by nineteen men who turned commercial airliners into flying bombs with nothing more sophisticated than fear and a few penknives.

At that moment of intense reflection, it seemed the only real path to world peace and security would be a return to basics. This attack made a mockery of the global arms race. Our only real hope of securing stability was in working to rebalance the Earth so that all human beings might live with dignity, free from want and fear. To achieve this, all religions and political ideologies throughout the world needed to reaffirm their commitment to a shared vision of a world of diversity founded on universal principles of justice and human rights. The Christian world, it seems, needed to re-examine the summation of the Ten Commandments that the Nazarene carpenter expressed as: 'You must love God and your neighbour as yourself.' The central tenet of this commandment was love of one's neighbour, and, as such, it was the bridge between God and all humankind. It was a commandment that carried huge political and social responsibilities. Jesus didn't simply define our neighbour as the person who lives next door; as the parable of the Good Samaritan demonstrates (Luke 10:29–37), our neighbours include so-called 'foreigners' and people of other beliefs.

As we turned a corner Agent McComiskey directed my attention to St Peter's Church, a large neoclassical midget, even in a landscape without the Twin Towers. Its fibreglass-shingle roof and windowsills were coated by the white storm that erupted with the collapse. Gaily coloured stained-glass windows, miraculously intact, offered a welcome relief from the lake of sorrow just off its western shore.

I stood for a moment, transfixed between two worlds — contemplating the power of good and evil, love and hate. I recalled part of a reflection I wrote in 1979 at Dachau Concentration Camp, Germany:

> Here is the power of evil.
> Where love is lost
> Distorted minds twist truth
> And desecrate God's image.

When man becomes a god
God protect his fellow man.

Juxtaposed with the cruelty of this attack were the unselfish and heroic accounts of hundreds of firemen and police officers who died in the act of saving others. I had listened earlier that day to an employee who had worked in the North Tower emotionally describing his frantic escape from the ninetieth floor along one of the evacuation stairwells. When he reached the thirtieth level, he began to meet firemen ascending with heavy oxygen equipment, pausing to catch their breath before continuing their climb towards hell.

It was to honour their memory and to give thanks for their selfless humanity that I had wanted to come to St Peter's. As I ascended the eleven granite steps of the church, passing between six columns, I thought of the five men who had carried Fr Judge's remains from the Twin Towers. They included two firemen, a police officer, a civilian and an agent from the Office of Emergency Management. One of the five, Fireman Zachary Vause of Engine Company 21, told me that, seconds before Fr Judge's body was lifted, the South Tower collapsed, turning the sun-drenched morning into night. He and others searched around in the blackness of the choking dust and grime and located Fr Judge's body. They lifted him onto an aluminium chair and raced in the direction of an ambulance somewhere near St Peter's. When they reached it, they found injured people on board who took priority over the dead. It was decided, however, that Fr Judge could not be left on a sidewalk. He was, therefore, carried up these same granite steps, through the main doors and up the aisle to the altar, before which rescuers reverently laid his body. Those who carried him paused for a moment to say a prayer before rushing out to continue their increasingly precarious rescue mission.

I knelt at the spot where Fr Judge had been laid. It was holy ground. I thought of the loyalty and esteem those firefighters had for their beloved chaplain, who gave his life for them. Whenever they were in danger, Fr Judge was beside them. When tragedy struck, he was there to comfort their widows and children. He was part of the fabric of their existence and, dead or alive, he was too precious to abandon. In the midst of an erupting hell, they brought him to God's altar and, in so doing, affirmed that good will ultimately triumph over evil.

Agent McComiskey, whom I now considered a friend, was standing a few feet behind me. As I rose and faced him, I remembered our first moment of connection — the name of St Thérèse of Lisieux, just thirty minutes before. I said to him, 'I bet you, Terry, there is a picture of St Thérèse somewhere in this church.' I don't know why I said that, but I somehow felt her presence.

'I bet there is,' he answered; and, in a matter of seconds, he exclaimed, 'There she is!' He pointed to the back of the altar on the west side, the place closest to the devastation without. It was a most beautiful marble statue, set into a permanent alcove. I approached it and touched the sprig of roses and crucifix she cradled. It somehow seemed appropriate that this short but epic journey, which had begun with her name, should end in her presence.

Just before I left St Peter's I noticed that the statue counterbalancing her on the east side of the altar was of St Patrick, delicately presenting a shamrock between his right thumb and index finger. Fr Mychal, baptised Robert Emmet Judge on 11 May 1933, loved his Irish roots. It seemed only right that his first resting-place should have been before the altar of God, guarded by Ireland's patron and a little French saint whose sacred relics had only recently been venerated by millions throughout the island home of his parents.

Don Mullan
Dublin, 2001

'... *a soul that is burning with love cannot remain inactive.*'
Thérèse of Lisieux

Appendix 1

The Worldwide Journey of the Reliquary of St Thérèse

The origins of the epic journey of Thérèse's sacred relics lie in her desire to be a missionary and a wish she expressed in her autobiography:

> I would like to travel over the whole earth to proclaim the Gospel on all five continents and even in the most remote isles. I would be a missionary.

With the publication of *Story of a Soul* in 1898, devotion to the young saint began. Increasingly, crowds flocked to her grave at the Municipal Cemetery in Lisieux, where she had been buried on 4 October 1897. There she remained, in the Carmelite plot, until 1923, when, on the occasion of her Beatification, her mortal remains were re-interred at the Carmel chapel, Lisieux.

The first pilgrimage of Thérèse's sacred relics occurred in 1947, the fiftieth anniversary of her death. On that occasion they were brought to almost every diocese of France. By then Thérèse had been declared Patroness of the Missions and Secondary Patroness of France, equal to St Joan of Arc.

With the advent of the centenary of her death (1997) the current pilgrimage of her relics began. Following is a list of countries the reliquary has visited, followed by places soon to be visited:

17–27 November 1995
Belgium

18–20 May 1996
Luxembourg

11 May–16 June 1996
Belgium

6–12 August 1996
Germany

20–25 August 1996
Italy

6–26 October 1997
Italy (Doctorate in Rome)

3–15 November 1997
Switzerland

15–24 November 1997
Austria

25–27 November 1997
Slovenia

13 December 1997–20 December 1998
Brazil

20 January–21 February 1999
Netherlands

27 February–5 May 1999
Russia and Siberia

5 May–30 June 1999
Kazakhstan

7 July–4 October 1999
Argentina

4 October 1999–30 January 2000
United States of America

30 January–2 April 2000
Philippines

2–14 April 2000

Taiwan

14–17 April 2000

Hong Kong

17–29 April 2000

Philippines

4 May–Christmas 2000

Italy

January–March 2001

Mexico

15 April (Easter Sunday)–2 July 2001

Ireland

15–23 July 2001

Bosnia-Herzegovina

September–December 2001

Canada

May–July 2002

French Polynesia, New Caledonia, Tahiti, Marquesas, Wallis and Futuna

August–October 2002

Middle East: Lebanon, Syria and Egypt

End 2002–2003

Indian Ocean: Réunion, Seychelles and Mauritius

2003

Spain, Central America, Scotland

2003–2004

Africa

'… it is only love that makes us acceptable to God.'

Thérèse of Lisieux

Appendix 2

Ireland's Pilgrimage of Grace

Below is the list of official veneration venues:

Easter Saturday, 14 April 2001
Departure from Basilica of St Thérèse, Lisieux, France

Easter Sunday, 15 April
Arrival at Rosslare aboard Irish Ferries MV *Normandy*
Parish Church, Rosslare Harbour, Co. Wexford
St Aidan's Cathedral, Enniscorthy, Co. Wexford

16 April
Bride Street Church, Wexford
Convent of the Adoration Sisters, Wexford

17 April
St Mary's Church, Cushinstown, Co. Wexford
Parish Church, New Ross, Co. Wexford
Carmelite Sisters, New Ross, Co. Wexford

18 April
Parish Church, Ferns, Co. Wexford
St Michael's Parish Church, Gorey, Co. Wexford

19 April
Carmelite Priory, Knocktopher, Co. Kilkenny

20 April
St Mary's Cathedral, Kilkenny

21 April
Carmelite Sisters, Kilmacud, Dublin

22 April
Carmelite Church, Beaumont, Dublin

23 April

Carmelite Sisters, Roebuck, Dublin

24 April

Bishop Rogan Park, Kilcullen, Co. Kildare

Cathedral of the Assumption, Carlow

25 April

Poor Clares, Carlow

St Teresa's Gardens, Donore Avenue, Dublin

St James's Hospital, Dublin

26 April

Carmelite Sisters, Hampton Carmel, Drumcondra, Dublin

27 April

Theresian Trust, 'Hampton', Drumcondra, Dublin

28 April

Knights of St Columbanus, Ely Place, Dublin

Carmelite Sisters, Delgany, Co. Wicklow

29 April

Loreto Abbey, Foxrock, Dublin

Carmelite Priory, Gort Muire, Ballinteer, Dublin

30 April

St Mary's Pro-Cathedral, Dublin

1 May

Carmelite Sisters, Malahide, Dublin

2 May

Legion of Mary, Brunswick Street, Dublin

3 May

Apostolic Nunciature, Navan Road, Dublin

Assisi House, Navan Road, Dublin

Carmelite Priory, Terenure College, Dublin

4 May

Mountjoy Prison, Dublin (Male and Female Wings)

5 May

St Colmcille's Carmelite Church, Knocklyon, Dublin

6–7 May

Avila Carmelite Retreat Centre, Donnybrook, Dublin

8–9 May

The Royal Hospital, Dublin

St Mary's Centre for the Visually Impaired, Dublin

St Teresa's Carmelite Church, Clarendon Street, Dublin

10–11 May

Irish Army Veneration, St Brigid's Garrison Church, Curragh Camp, Co. Kildare

White Abbey Carmelite Church, Kildare

12 May

De La Salle Brothers, Kildare

Cross Keys, Claregate Street, Kildare

St Brigid's Parish Church, Kildare

Presentation Convent, Kildare

The Louis and Zélie Martin Hospice, Blackrock, Dublin

Our Lady's Manor, Bullock Castle, Dalkey, Dublin

The Poor Clares, Simmonscourt Road, Ballsbridge, Dublin

13 May

Church of St Teresa, Mount Merrion, Dublin

St Joseph's Carmelite Church, Berkeley Road, Dublin

14–15 May

Church of Our Lady of Mount Carmel, Whitefriar Street, Dublin

16 May

Our Lady's Hospice, Harold's Cross, Dublin

Carmelite Sisters, Firhouse, Dublin

17 May

St James's Church, Athboy, Co. Meath

Charity of Jesus and Mary Sisters, Residential Home for the Mentally Handicapped, Delvin, Co. Westmeath

Little Flower Church, Brotenstown, Co. Westmeath

Cathedral of Christ the King, Mullingar, Co. Westmeath

18 May

St Mel's Cathedral, Longford Town

19 May

Church of Ireland, Moate, Co. Westmeath

St Patrick's Carmelite Church, Moate, Co. Westmeath

20 May

Medical Missionaries of Mary, Drogheda, Co. Louth

21 May

Cathedral of SS Patrick and Felim, Cavan Town

22 May

Parish of Ballinagh, Kilmore, Co. Cavan

Holy Trinity Norbertine Abbey, Kilnacrott, Ballyjamesduff, Co. Cavan

23 May

Killinkere Parish, Co. Cavan

Parish Church, Cooley Peninsula, Co. Louth

Cathedral of SS Patrick and Colman, Newry, Co. Down

Carmelite Sisters, Glenvale, Co. Down

24 May

St Peter's Church, Shankill, Lurgan, Co. Down

25 May

St Patrick's Cathedral, Armagh

26 May

Ballybay, Co. Monaghan

St Macartan's Cathedral, Monaghan Town

Ascension Sunday, 27 May

St Peter's Cathedral, Belfast, Co. Antrim

28 May

Redemptorist Monastery, Clonard, Belfast, Co. Antrim

29 May

St Paul's Church, Falls Road, Belfast, Co. Antrim

Poor Clare Convent, Cliftonville Road, Belfast, Co. Antrim

Unity Flats, Belfast, Co. Antrim

Holy Cross Passionist Church, Ardoyne, Belfast, Co. Antrim

30 May

Cistercian Monastery, Portglenone, Co. Antrim

St Eugene's Cathedral, Derry

31 May

Carmelite Monastery, Termonbacca, Creggan, Derry

1 June

Cathedral of SS Eunan and Columba, Letterkenny, Co. Donegal

2 June

Parish Church, Falcarragh, Co. Donegal

Pentecost Sunday, 3 June

Gortahork Parish, Co. Donegal

Loughanure Parish, Annagry, Co. Donegal

Dunloe, Co. Donegal

Glenties (scene of 1913 St Thérèse miracle), Co. Donegal

Church of SS Joseph and Conal, Bruckless, Co. Donegal

4 June

Mountcharles Parish, Co. Donegal

Ballyshannon, Co. Donegal

Church of St Thérèse, Ballintogher, Co. Sligo

St Mary's Cathedral, Sligo

5 June

St Muredach's Cathedral, Ballina, Co. Mayo

6 June

Carrocastle Parish Church, Ballaghaderreen, Co. Roscommon

Cathedral of the Annunciation and St Nathy, Ballaghaderreen,
   Roscommon

7 June

Dunmore Parish Church, Co. Galway

Cathedral of the Assumption, Tuam, Co. Galway

8 June

Williamstown Parish Church, Co. Galway

Tranquilla Carmelite Convent, Knock, Co. Mayo

9–10 June

National Shrine of Our Lady, Knock, Co. Mayo

11 June

Athenry Parish Church, Co. Galway

Carmelite Abbey, Loughrea, Co. Galway

12 June

St Joseph Carmelite Convent, Loughrea, Co. Galway

13 June

St Brendan's Cathedral, Loughrea, Co. Galway

14 June

Parish Church, Barna, Co. Galway

Cill Éinne Church, Spiddal, Co. Galway

Convent of the Poor Clares, Nun's Island, Co. Galway

Cathedral of Our Lady Assumed into Heaven and St Nicholas, Galway

15 June

Cathedral of SS Peter and Paul, Ennis, Co. Clare

16 June

Poor Clares Convent, St Francis Street, Ennis, Co. Clare

16–17 June

St Joseph's Carmelite Monastery, Tallow, Co. Waterford

18 June

St John's Cathedral, Limerick

19 June

Limerick Prison

St Mary's Cathedral, Killarney, Co. Kerry

20 June

Macroom, Co. Cork

Cathedral of SS Mary and Anne, Cork

21 June

Cork Prison

Poor Clares Convent, College Road, Cork

St Colman's Cathedral, Cobh, Co. Cork

22 June

Benedictine Convent, Cobh, Co. Cork

Carmelite Monastery, Castlemartyr, Co. Cork

23 June

St Mary's Parish Church, Carrigtwohill, Co. Cork

SMA Church, Blackrock, Cork

24 June

Carmelite Priory, Kinsale, Co. Cork

25 June

Church of the Nativity of the Blessed Virgin Mary, Doneraile, Co. Cork

Cathedral of the Assumption, Thurles, Co. Tipperary

26 June

St Mary's Church, Ballyneale, Carrick-on-Suir, Co. Tipperary

Holy Trinity Cathedral, Waterford

27 June

St Patrick's Hospital, Waterford

St Patrick's Purgatory, Lough Derg, Co. Donegal

Gormanston Army Camp, Co. Meath

Visitation Monastery, Stamullen, Co. Westmeath

28 June

Nazareth House, Malahide Road, Dublin

St Brigid's Hospice, The Curragh, Co. Kildare

Dara Park, Kildare Town

Opus Dei, Barrow House, Monasterevin, Co. Kildare

Cistercian Abbey, Roscrea, Co. Tipperary

29 June

Parish Church, Abbeyleix, Co. Laois

St Dympna's Psychiatric Hospital, Carlow

Kent Engineering, Wexford Industrial Estate, Wexford

Our Lady's Island

30 June

Clonard Parish Church, Wexford Town

1 July
Thanksgiving Celebration, Wexford GAA Park
St Patrick's Church, Rosslare Harbour, Co. Wexford
2 July
Departure from Rosslare aboard Irish Ferries MV *Normandy*
3 July
Arrival at the Basilica of St Thérèse, Lisieux, France

In addition to the above scheduled venues, there were 183 stops in response to knots of people — including many sick people — at a variety of points on the roads between venues. According to Fr Ryan, 'this proved to be a wonderful and unexpected feature of the entire pilgrimage'.

Acknowledgements

I am indebted to a great many people for their help in producing this book. In the first instance I am deeply indebted to Father J. Linus Ryan O.Carm., National Co-ordinator, St Thérèse's Relics Irish Visit. His kindness, patience and openness were, at all times, a privilege to encounter.

Immense gratitude is also due to Bernie Bergin, Kilkenny, whose secretarial assistance, research skills and great good humour were, at all times, a delight to encounter. As one of the wounded of the Dublin and Monaghan bombings, she is an inspiration to all who seek truth and justice on this island. I am especially indebted to her husband John and daughters Jenny and Emily (and Nicky) for their support and patience.

Continuing gratitude is also expressed to my good friend, John Scally, for his support and advice.

My gratitude is also owed to many Carmelite Sisters who, by their prayers, letters and telephone calls, were of immense help and encouragement. These include: Sister Brigeen, Sister Mary John and all the Sisters of the Kilmacud Carmel; Sister Immaculata and Sister Thérèse, Hampton Carmel; Sister Monica, Delgany Carmel; Sister Anne, New Ross Carmel; Sister M. Peter, Convent of Perpetual

Adoration, Wexford; and Mother John of the Cross and the sisters of St Thérèse of Lisieux Carmel, Loretto, Pennsylvania.

Pat Sweeney, Jim Doyle and Liam O'Keeffe, driver and co-drivers of the 'Thérèsemobile', became, during the course of producing this book, good and genuine friends. I am sincerely grateful to them.

Over 170 submissions were sent for consideration. Unfortunately, not all could be included. I gratefully acknowledge the contributions of the following: Gregory Allen (RIP), Vera Ambrose, A.B, Colman, Alice, Peter, H.P.K., KM(H), J. McC., P, V. McD, Mary, Marce, Ann, Katharine, Jim & Deborah, Joe, Tom Atkins, Martina Aughney, John Aughney, Sean Beattie, Mary Bergin, Brother Columbanus, Mary Bradley, M. Brogan, Sister Mairéad Brophy, Breda Browne, Theresa Buckley, Kathleen Buckley, Tracey Buckley, Gerry Burns, Michael Burns, Agnes Carley, Maura Cathcart, Thomas Comiskey, Bishop Brendan Comiskey, Noleen Connell, Lelia Considine, Betty & Michael Cooke, Annette Cummins, Carmel Cunningham, Cristin Dalton, Deacy/Smyth, Kathleen Delaney, Betty Dillon, Patrick Donoghue, Marie Doyle, Noreen Dunne, Sarah Factor, Frances Feehely, Noreen Fitzgerald, Frank Flanagan, Caitríona Fogarty, Bill Fogarty, Noelle Fogarty, Shauna Forbes, Geraldine Forde, Eileen Forde, Mary Gallagher, Geraldine Gallagher, Margaret Gallagher O'Brien, James K. Gardiner, Catherine Gerety, Mary Golden, Father Eltin Griffin, Joe Heffernan, Sister Finian Hegarty, Kitty Hennessy, Maura Henry, Ann Hoban, Jack Hynes, Father Dominic Johnson OSB, Bridie Jones, Bridie Kavanagh, Josephine Kealy, Myra Kearney, Phil Kehoe, Dermot Kelly, Dr Deirdre Killelea, Father John Lawler, Anne Lennon, Emma Niamh and Katrina Lennon, Tess Lovell, Betty Lynch,

Rosaleen Lyons, Aideen Madden, Noel Magnier, Father Michael Maher SM, Florence Mahony, Peg Mallon, Eileen Marley, C. Martin, Annie Massey, Florence McCabe, May McClintock, Father Gerard McCloskey, Francis McDonagh (11), George McDonnell, Ann McGahey, Teenie McGarry, James McGlynn, Joseph McKenna, Joan McKeon, Amanda McKinley, Pat McLucas, Esther McManus, Father Damian McNeice, Carmel Meade, Geraldine Melia, Alina Millard, Mary Frances Mooney, Sister Gabriella Morgan, Father Richard Mulcahy, Angela Mulcahy, Frances J. Mullen, Anna Mullin, Marie Nesney, Clara Ní Ghiolla, Annia Ní Scanlon, Ann O'Brien, Aiden O'Brien, Patrick O'Connor, Vincent O'Connor, Kathleen O'Connor, Michael O'Connor, Mary D. O'Connor, Bridie O'Grady, Father Jim O'Halloran, Margaret Mary O'Mahony, Margaret O'Neill, Breda O'Neill, Brian & Josephine O'Reilly, Alacoque O'Reilly, Angela O'Rourke, Monica O'Shea, Bernadette O'Sullivan, Mary O'Sullivan, Marcella Owens, Bernie Power, John & Eileen Quinn, Pat Regan, Joan Rigney, Seamus Scally, John Sherry, Geraldine Sinnott, N.M. Smith, Sister Isabelle Smyth, Sister Immaculata, Sister Mary Cecilia, Sister Ann, Sister Gwen of the Holy Spirit, Sister Patricia FSM, Sister Brenda Swan, Dr M.A. Tierney, Malachy Toal, Iris Toner, Frank Travers, Soline Vatinel, Patrick Walsh, Daire Whelan, Eilish White, Gary White Deer and Tony Woulfe.

Bishop Brendan Comiskey; Bishop Patrick Ahern and his gracious secretary, Peggy Peet, St Thomas More Church, New York; Noel Smyth, Father Eltin Griffin O.Carm; Father Eugene McCaffrey OCD; and Father Damian McNeice contributed in their own special ways to the birth of this publication.

I am indebted to many colleagues in the media who helped me with this project, particularly in the initial stages. They include:

Rachel Andrews, *Sunday Tribune*; Michelle Booker, *Irish Mirror*; Mark Cagney, *Ireland AM*, TV3; Fintan Deere, Sean Doherty, Highland Radio; Michael Doyle, *Irish Mirror*; Fintan Duffy, Northern Sound Radio; Joe Duffy, RTÉ; Frank Flanagan, South-East Radio; Frank Galligan; Eithne Hande, *The Sunday Show*, RTÉ; Garrett Harte, Producer, *20/20*, TV3; Conor Kavanagh, *Irish Star*; Lorraine Keane, *Ireland AM*, TV3; Mark Little, RTÉ; Robin Livingstone, *Andersonstown News*; Paul Maguire, LMFM Radio; Patsy McGarry, *The Irish Times*; Seamus McKinney, *Irish News*; Mark McLaren, *Cork Evening Echo*; J. Leo McMahon, *Southern Star*; Mick McNiffe, *Irish Mirror*; Fiona Mitchell, TV3 News; Jane Murphy, LMFM Radio; Larissa Nolan, *Sunday World*; Niall O'Connor, *Irish Star*; Caroline Orr, Highland Radio; Donncha Ó Dúlaing, RTÉ; Gerry Ryan, 2FM, RTÉ; John Tumelty, *Andersonstown News*; Joe Walsh, *Ireland AM*, TV3; Ken Whelan, *Ireland on Sunday*.

I am indebted to the following publications and media outlets: *Andersonstown News*, *Armagh Parish Bulletin*, *Beaumont Parish Bulletin*, *Cathedral Bulletin Thurles*, *Anglo Celt*, *Derry Journal*, Highland Radio, *Ireland AM*, TV3, *Ireland on Sunday*, *Kilkenny People*, *Leitrim Observer*, *Limerick Leader*, LMFM Radio, *Nenagh Guardian*, Northern Sound Radio, *SMA Magazine*, *St Eunan's Cathedral, Letterkenny, Newsletter*, *Marino Parish, Dublin, Newsletter*, *Pettigo Parish Newsletter*, *The Gerry Ryan Show*, RTÉ, *Irish Independent*, *Irish Mirror*, *Irish News*, *Irish World*, *Newsletter*, *Southern Star*, *The Sunday Show*, RTÉ, *Sunday Tribune*, *Sunday World*.

My gratitude is also extended to the following friends, helpers and associates: Father Paddy Kelly and St Patrick's Missionary Society, Kiltegan, including Fathers Paddy Hagan and Neil Blaney; Aude Catala, Paris; Laurence Quesney, International Centre, Basilica of St Thérèse, Lisieux; Br Bryan Paquette OCD, Washington, for kind permission to quote from the translation of *Story of a Soul* by the late John Clarke, OCD; Barry Pimlott; Tony O'Byrne; Madeline O'Shaugnessy of Irish Ferries, Teresa Gleeson, John Kelly, Micky McKinney; Bernadine Stanley, Archbishop Desmond Tutu, South Africa; Brian Meagher in whose Manhattan apartment much of the Introduction was written; Todd and Helen Allen, New Jersey; Richard Moore; Desmond J. Doherty; John Coyle, Sister Kathleen and Dr Annie Deignan, New York; Kit DeFever; Emma Coakley; Amelia Penny, Clare Barry, Frank Massey, Brothers Jack Driscoll and Harry Dunkak, New York; Sister Mary Anne Dillon, Sister Virginia Bertschi, Sister Charlene Kelly, the Sisters at McAuley Hall, Dr Dan Fredricks and Patricia McNelis and the staff of Mount Aloysius College, Cresson, Pennsylvania; Sister Helen Prejean, Louisiana; Shirley Hixson, Pittsburgh; Owen Rodgers, New York; Steve Reichi, Communications Department, American Museum of Natural History, New York; Captain Mike Currid, Fire Department New York; Second Officer John O'Connor and Leading Fire Officer Chris Maverley, Cork Fire Brigade; Fr Pat McCafferty, Belfast; Clare Reilly, Mark Thompson and Andrée Murphy, Belfast; Maureen and Dermot Beatty, Dublin; Kyran O'Neill; Esther Buckley, Cork; Richard Campbell; Liz Curtis; Eoin O'Mara, James Doyle and Noel Clarke of Crumlin Sorting Office; Mary Ellen, Parochial House, Letterkenny; Michael Farrelly, Indigo; Gemma Jordan; Kieran Joyce, Cork; Father Bertie O'Mahony, Farrenree, Cork; Father Michael Seery, Ballygawley, Co. Tyrone; Nell and Tom Smith, Perrystown, Dublin; Gary White Deer, Oklahoma; Father Gearóid Walsh, Adm. St Mary's Cathedral, Killarney; Terrence McComiskey, Staten Island; Father Michael Duffy OFM, Philadelphia; Father Kevin Madigan, Adm.

St Peter's Church, Manhattan; Firefighter Zachary Vause, Engine Company 21, New York; Erika Lutzner; Joe Murray; Fr Don Redden, Anthuanette Hidalgo and Maraeiana Haspil, Hispanic Mission, Fort Pierce, Florida; Olivia Walsh, Paul Greengrass, Mark Redhead and Lucy Dykes.

My thanks to the staff of Wolfhound Press, especially Seamus Cashman for his continuing support and encouragement. Also David Houlden, Susan Jefferies, Maria Farren and special thanks to my editor, Tana Eilís French, and the Wolfhound Managing Editor, Emer Ryan.

Finally, I wish to thank my siblings and their families for their continuing support: Moya, Liam, Margaret, Cathal, Susan and Deirdre; and, last but not least, those whose love, friendship, encouragement and support I so often feel unworthy of: Margaret, Thérèse, Carl and Emma. Immense gratitude must also be expressed to a special family friend, Thérèse Martin.

No doubt I have forgotten many who richly deserve to be remembered with gratitude. For those whom I have inadvertently omitted, I ask their understanding and forgiveness.

Index of Contributors

'There were so many things to say that
I couldn't say anything at all,
my heart was too full.'

Thérèse of Lisieux